MINISTERS OF THE CROWN

MINISTERS OF THE CROWN

D.A.Pickrill

ROUTLEDGE & KEGAN PAUL
London, Boston and Henley

First published in 1981
by Routledge & Kegan Paul Ltd
39 Store Street,
London WC1E 7DD,
9 Park Street,
Boston, Mass. 02108, USA and
Broadway House,
Newtown Road,
Henley-on-Thames,
Oxon RG9 1EN
Printed in Great Britain by
Thomson Litho Ltd
East Kilbride, Scotland

ISBN   0 7100 0916 X

CONTENTS

INTRODUCTION

This book lists, in accessible form, holders of ministerial posts, senior and junior, in most cases from the earliest known date.

It appears that at present there is not any single work in which this information can be found; only 'Haydn's Book of Dignities', now nearly a century old, has attempted anything similar. There are, of course, many lists of holders of the major offices and a number of works cover the complete range of offices over a limited period; there are, too, studies covering the work and personnel of individual departments.

The lists have been checked with the works listed in the Bibliography, which frequently differ amongst themselves and, where necessary, confirmation has been obtained from the department concerned. As scarcely any of the works consulted have been correct throughout it can hardly be hoped that the present volume is free from fault; the author would be grateful to have any errors or omissions brought to his attention.

As the intention has been to list the ministers of the central government, the offices concerned with Ireland have been shown only from the holders in office in 1801.

For those offices which date from the sixteenth century or earlier the dates shown are no doubt in many cases the date by which the minister was known to be in office rather than the date of his appointment. In a few cases the nature of the office has changed to such an extent that the listing has commenced with the first holder of the office bearing any resemblance to its later form. There were, for instance, Admirals in early times but the office of Lord High Admiral as a political office rather than a fleet commander would appear to date from the appointment of Lord Russell in 1540. So too with the Lord President of the Council; the office in anything like its present form dates from the reform of the Privy Council in 1679.

In the case of the junior ministers it should not be supposed that, in the eighteenth century and sometimes well into the nineteenth, an under-secretary was necessarily a politician, a junior minister in the modern sense. He may have been; he may equally well have been in present-day terms a civil servant or a member of his minister's personal staff.

Although the Speaker of the House of Commons is not a minister, at least in modern times, a list of the holders of the office has been included as it may be found to be of use.

If an office has been vacant due to a delay in making a new appointment this has been indicated only where the gap has been significant.

As the intention is to show who held a particular office at any given date it has been regarded as necessary to distinguish between persons of similar name or peers holding the same title only where confusion has seemed likely to arise as, for instance, with the three Marquesses of Salisbury who were Lords Privy Seal within some fifty years. Equally, ministers whose name or title changed have been indicated only where they served more than one period of office in the same post. The full career of the great majority of the persons in this book can, of course, be found in the 'Dictionary of National Biography' or 'Who's Who'.

Lastly, I should like to offer my thanks to the staffs of libraries, record offices and government departments who have helped with answers to my queries.

BIBLIOGRAPHY

BALL, Francis Elrington, 'The Judges in Ireland 1221-1921', 1926.
BUTLER, David and SLOMAN, Anne, 'British Political Facts 1900-1979', 5th edn, 1980.
COOK, Chris and KEITH, Brendan, 'British Historical Facts 1830-1900', 1975.
COOK, Chris and STEVENSON, John, 'British Historical Facts 1760-1830', 1980.
CHESTER, D.N. and WILLSON, F.M.G., 'The Organisation of British Central Government 1914-1956', 1957.
'Dictionary of National Biography'.
'Dod's Parliamentary Companion'.
'Haydn's Book of Dignities'.
'Keesing's Contemporary Archives'.
POWELL, Ken and COOK, Chris, 'English Historical Facts 1485-1603', 1977.
POWICKE, F.M. and FRYDE, E.B., 'Handbook of British Chronology', 1961.
SAINTY, J.C., 'Office Holders in Modern Britain', from 1972.
SOMERVILLE, Sir Robert, 'Office Holders in the Duchy and County Palatine of Lancaster', 1972.
STENTON, M., 'Who's Who of British Members of Parliament', from 1976.
UNDERHILL, Nicholas, 'The Lord Chancellor', 1978.
'Who's Who' and 'Who Was Who'.
WILDING, Norman and LAUNDY, Philip, 'Encyclopedia of Parliament', 4th edn, 1972.
WILLIAMS, William Rees, 'Official Lists of the Duchy and County Palatine of Lancaster', 1901.

PRIME MINISTER, TREASURY AND ECONOMIC AFFAIRS

PRIME MINISTER

1721	Sir Robert Walpole	1827	Viscount Goderich
1742	Earl of Wilmington	1828	Duke of Wellington
1743	Henry Pelham	1830	Earl Grey
1754	Duke of Newcastle	1834	Viscount Melbourne
1756	Duke of Devonshire	1834	Duke of Wellington
1757	Duke of Newcastle	1834	Sir Robert Peel
1762	Earl of Bute	1835	Viscount Melbourne
1763	George Grenville	1841	Sir Robert Peel
1765	Marquess of Rockingham	1846	Lord John Russell
1766	Earl of Chatham	1852	Earl of Derby
1767	Duke of Grafton	1852	Earl of Aberdeen
1770	Lord North	1855	Viscount Palmerston
1782	Marquess of Rockingham	1858	Earl of Derby
1782	Earl of Shelburne	1858	Viscount Palmerston
1783	Duke of Portland	1865	Earl (formerly Lord John) Russell
1783	William Pitt		
1801	Henry Addington	1866	Earl of Derby
1804	William Pitt	1868	Benjamin Disraeli
1806	Lord Grenville	1868	William Ewart Gladstone
1807	Duke of Portland	1874	Benjamin Disraeli
1809	Spencer Perceval	1880	William Ewart Gladstone
1812	Earl of Liverpool	1885	Marquess of Salisbury
1827	George Canning	1886	William Ewart Gladstone

1886	Marquess of Salisbury	1945	Clement Attlee
1892	William Ewart Gladstone	1951	Winston Churchill
1894	Earl of Rosebery	1955	Sir Anthony Eden
1895	Marquess of Salisbury	1957	Harold Macmillan
1902	Arthur Balfour	1963	Sir Alec Douglas-Home
1905	Sir Henry Campbell-Bannerman	1964	Harold Wilson
		1970	Edward Heath
1908	Herbert H.Asquith	1974	Harold Wilson
1916	David Lloyd George	1976	James Callaghan
1922	Andrew Bonar Law	1979	Margaret Thatcher
1923	Stanley Baldwin		
1924	James Ramsay MacDonald		
1924	Stanley Baldwin		
1929	James Ramsay MacDonald		
1935	Stanley Baldwin		
1937	Neville Chamberlain		
1940	Winston Churchill		

MINISTER FOR THE CIVIL SERVICE

Since 1968 the Prime Minister has also held the post of Minister for the Civil Service.

MINISTER OF STATE

1974   Robert Sheldon
1974   Charles Morris
1979   Paul Channon
1981   Bernard Hayhoe

PARLIAMENTARY SECRETARY (1970-4)

1970	David Howell	1972-4	Geoffrey Johnson-Smith
1972-4	Kenneth Baker	1974	John Grant

TREASURERS, LORD HIGH TREASURERS, FIRST LORDS OF THE TREASURY

1156	William	1329	Robert Wodehouse
1159	Richard FitzNeal	1330	William Melton
1196	William of Ely	1331	William Airmyn
1217	Eustace of Fauconberg	1332	Robert Ayleston
1228	Walter Mauclerc	1334	Richard Bury
1233	Peter des Rivaux	1334	Henry Burghersh
1234	Hugh Pateshull	1337	William de la Zouche
1240	William Haverhill	1338	Robert Wodehouse
1252	Philip Lovel	1338	William de la Zouche
1258	John Crakehall	1340	Sir Robert Sadington
1260	John of Caux	1340	Roger Northburgh
1263	Nicholas of Ely	1341	Sir Robert Parvyng
1263	Henry, Prior of St Radegund	1341	William Cusance
		1344	William Edington
1265	Thomas Wymondham	1356	John Sheppey
1270	John Chishull	1360	Simon Langham
1271	Philip of Eye	1363	John Barnet
1273	Joseph Chauncy	1369	Thomas Brantingham
1280	Richard Ware	1371	Lord Scrope of Bolton
1284	John Kirkby	1375	Sir Robert Ashton
1290	William March	1377	Henry Wakefield
1295	Walter Langton	1377	Thomas Brantingham
1307	Walter Reynolds	1381	Sir Robert Hales
1310	John Sandall	1381	Sir Hugh Segrave
1312	Walter Langton	1386	John Fordham
1314	Walter Norwich	1386	John Gilbert
1317	John Hotham	1389	Thomas Brantingham
1318	John Waldwayn	1389	John Gilbert
1318	John Sandall	1391	John Waltham
1320	Walter Stapeldon	1395	Roger Walden
1325	William Melton	1398	Guy Mone
1326	John Stratford	1398	Earl of Wiltshire
1327	Adam Orleton	1399	John Norbury
1327	Henry Burghersh	1401	Laurence Allerthorp
1328	Thomas Charlton	1402	Henry Bowet

1402	Guy Mone	1470	Earl of Worcester
1403	Lord Roos of Helmsley	1470	Sir John Langstrother
1404	Lord Furnival	1471	Earl of Essex (formerly
1407	Nicholas Bubwith		Viscount Bourchier)
1408	Sir John Tiptoft	1483	Sir John Wood
1410	Lord Scrope of Masham	1484	Lord Audley
1411	Sir John Pelham	1486	Lord Dynham
1413	Earl of Arundel	1501	Earl of Surrey (Duke of
1416	Sir Hugh Mortimer		Norfolk from 1514)
1416	Sir Roger Leche	1522	Duke of Norfolk (son of
1416	Lord FitzHugh		above)
1421	William Kinwolmarsh	1547	Duke of Somerset
1422	John Stafford	1550	Marquess of Winchester
1426	Lord Hungerford	1572	Lord Burghley
1432	Lord Scrope of Masham	1599	Lord Buckhurst (Earl of
1433	Lord Cromwell		Dorset from 1604)
1443	Lord Sudley	1608	Earl of Salisbury
1446	Marmaduke Lumley	1612	Earl of Northampton
1449	Lord Saye and Sele	1613	Lord Ellesmere
1450	Lord Beauchamp of Powick	1614	Earl of Suffolk
1452	Earl of Worcester	1618	George Abbot
1455	Earl of Ormond	1620	Viscount Mandeville
1455	Viscount Bourchier	1621	Lord Cranfield (Earl of
1456	Earl of Shrewsbury		Middlesex from 1622)
1458	Earl of Ormond	1624	Lord Ley (Earl of
1460	Viscount Bourchier		Marlborough from 1626)
1462	Earl of Worcester	1628	Lord Weston (Earl of
1463	Lord Grey of Ruthin		Portland from 1633)
1464	Walter Blount	1635	William Laud
1466	Earl Rivers	1636	William Juxon
1469	Sir John Langstrother	1641	Lord Lyttelton
1469	William Grey	1643	Lord Cottington

Under the Commonwealth the office was in commission

1660	Sir Edward Hyde	1660	Earl of Southampton

1667	Duke of Albemarle	1697	Charles Montagu
1670	Lord Ashley	1699	Earl of Tankerville
1672	Lord Clifford	1700	Lord Godolphin
1673	Earl of Danby	1701	Earl of Carlisle
1679	Earl of Essex	1702	Lord Godolphin (Earl of Godolphin from 1706)
1679	Laurence Hyde (Earl of Rochester from 1682)		
		1710	Earl Poulett
1684	Sidney Godolphin	1711	Earl of Oxford
1685	Earl of Rochester	1714	Duke of Shrewsbury
1687	Lord Belasyse	1714	Lord Halifax
1689	Viscount Mordaunt	1715	Earl of Carlisle
1690	Sir John Lowther	1715	Robert Walpole
1690	Lord (formerly Sidney) Godolphin	1717	Viscount Stanhope
		1718	Earl of Sunderland
1696	Sir Stephen Fox	1721	Robert Walpole

After this date the First Lord of the Treasury was also Prime Minister with the exception of the following:

1766-7	Duke of Grafton	1891-2	Arthur Balfour
1885-6	Lord Iddesleigh	1895-1902	Arthur Balfour
1886-91	W.H.Smith		

CHANCELLOR OF THE EXCHEQUER

The office of Chancellor of the Exchequer, founded in the reign of Henry III, was in early times a minor post and is listed here from the Restoration. In the eighteenth and early nineteenth centuries the post was on occasion held temporarily by the Chief Justice of the King's Bench and these are included.

1660	Sir Robert Long	1690	Richard Hampden
1667	Lord Ashley	1694	Lord Godolphin
1672	Sir John Duncombe	1695	Charles Montagu
1679	Laurence Hyde	1699	John Smith
1679	Sir John Ernle	1701	Henry Boyle
1689	Lord Delamere	1708	John Smith

1710	Robert Harley	1827	George Canning
1711	Robert Benson	1827	Lord Tenterden
1713	Sir William Wyndham	1827	J.C.Herries
1714	Sir Richard Onslow	1828	Henry Goulburn
1715	Robert Walpole	1830	Viscount Althorp
1717	James Stanhope	1834	Lord Denman
1718	John Aislabie	1834	Sir Robert Peel
1721	Sir John Pratt	1835	Thomas Spring Rice
1721	Sir Robert Walpole	1839	Francis Thornhill Baring
1742	Samuel Sandys	1841	Henry Goulburn
1743	Henry Pelham	1846	Charles Wood
1754	Sir William Lee	1852	Benjamin Disraeli
1754	Henry Bilson Legge	1852	William Ewart Gladstone
1755	Sir George Lyttelton	1855	Sir George Cornewall Lewis
1756	Henry Bilson Legge		
1757	Lord Mansfield	1858	Benjamin Disraeli
1757	Henry Bilson Legge	1859	William Ewart Gladstone
1761	Viscount Barrington	1866	Benjamin Disraeli
1762	Sir Francis Dashwood	1868	George Ward Hunt
1763	George Grenville	1868	Robert Lowe
1765	William Dowdeswell	1873	William Ewart Gladstone
1766	Charles Townshend	1874	Sir Stafford Northcote
1767	Lord Mansfield	1880	William Ewart Gladstone
1767	Lord North	1882	H.C.E.Childers
1782	Lord John Cavendish	1885	Sir Michael Hicks-Beach
1782	William Pitt	1886	Sir William Vernon Harcourt
1783	Lord John Cavendish		
1783	William Pitt	1886	Lord Randolph Churchill
1801	Henry Addington	1887	George J.Goschen
1804	William Pitt	1892	Sir William Vernon Harcourt
1806	Lord Ellenborough		
1806	Lord Henry Petty	1895	Sir Michael Hicks-Beach
1807	Spencer Perceval	1902	C.T.Ritchie
1812	Lord Ellenborough	1903	Austen Chamberlain
1812	Nicholas Vansittart	1905	Herbert H.Asquith
1823	Frederick Robinson	1908	David Lloyd George

1915	Reginald McKenna	1955	Harold Macmillan
1916	Andrew Bonar Law	1957	Peter Thorneycroft
1919	Austen Chamberlain	1958	Derick Heathcoat Amory
1921	Sir Robert Horne	1960	Selwyn Lloyd
1922	Stanley Baldwin	1962	Reginald Maudling
1923	Neville Chamberlain	1964	James Callaghan
1924	Philip Snowden	1967	Roy Jenkins
1924	Winston Churchill	1970	Iain Macleod
1929	Philip Snowden	1970	Anthony Barber
1931	Neville Chamberlain	1974	Denis Healey
1937	Sir John Simon	1979	Sir Geoffrey Howe
1940	Sir Kingsley Wood		
1943	Sir John Anderson		
1945	Hugh Dalton		
1947	Sir Stafford Cripps		
1950	Hugh Gaitskell		
1951	R.A.Butler		

THIRD LORD OF THE TREASURY (1868-9)

1868   James Stansfeld

SENIOR SECRETARY TO THE TREASURY (to 1830)
PARLIAMENTARY SECRETARY TO THE TREASURY (from 1830)

1660	Sir Philip Warwick	1756	Nicholas Hardinge
1667	Sir George Downing	1758	James West
1671	Sir Robert Howard	1762	Samuel Martin
1673	Charles Bertie	1763	Jeremiah Dyson
1679	Henry Guy	1763	Charles Jenkinson
1689	William Jephson	1765	William Mellish
1691	Henry Guy	1765	Charles Lowndes
1695	William Lowndes	1767	Grey Cooper
1724	John Scrope	1782	Henry Strachey
1752	James West	1782	Thomas Orde

1783	Richard Burke	1902	Sir Alexander Acland Hood
1783	George Rose	1905	George Whiteley
1801	John Hiley Addington	1908	Joseph Pease
1802	Nicholas Vansittart	1910	Master of Elibank
1804	William Sturges Bourne	1912	Percy Illingworth
1806	Nicholas Vansittart	1915	John Gulland
1807	Henry Wellesley	1915-16	John Gulland
1809	Charles Arbuthnot	1915-16	Lord Edmund Talbot
1823	Stephen Rumbold Lushington	1916-21	Lord Edmund Talbot
1827	Joseph Planta	1916-17	Neil Primrose
1830	Edward Ellice	1917-21	Frederick Guest
1832	Sir Charles Wood	1921-2	Charles McCurdy
1834	Sir George Clerk	1921-2	Leslie Wilson
1835	Edward John Stanley	1922	Leslie Wilson
1841	Sir Denis Le Marchant	1923	Bolton Eyres-Monsell
1841	Sir Thomas Fremantle	1924	Benjamin Spoor
1844	John Young	1924	Bolton Eyres-Monsell
1846	Henry Tufnell	1929	Thomas Kennedy
1850	William Goodenough Hayter	1931	Sir Bolton Eyres-Monsell
1852	William Forbes Mackenzie	1931	David Margesson
1853	William Goodenough Hayter	1940-40	David Margesson
1858	Sir William G. Hylton Jolliffe	1940-2	Sir Charles Edwards
		1941-5	James Stuart
1859	Henry B.W.Brand	1942-5	William Whiteley
1866	Thomas Edward Taylor	1945	James Stuart
1868	Gerard James Noel	1945	William Whiteley
1868	George Grenfell Glyn	1951	Patrick Buchan-Hepburn
1873	Arthur Wellesley Peel	1955	Edward Heath
1874	William Hart Dyke	1959	Martin Redmayne
1880	Lord Richard Grosvenor	1964	Edward Short
1885	Aretas Akers-Douglas	1966	John Silkin
1886	Arnold Morley	1969	Robert Mellish
1886	Aretas Akers-Douglas	1970	Francis Pym
1892	Edward Marjoribanks	1973	Humphrey Atkins
1894	Thomas Edward Ellis	1974	Robert Mellish
1895	Sir William Hood Walrond	1976	Michael Cocks

1979   Michael Jopling

JUNIOR SECRETARY TO THE TREASURY (1711-1830)
FINANCIAL SECRETARY TO THE TREASURY (since 1830)

1711	Thomas Harley	1802	John Sargent
1714	John Taylor	1804	William Huskisson
1715	Horatio Walpole	1806	John King
1717	Charles Stanhope	1806	William Henry Fremantle
1721	Horatio Walpole	1807	William Huskisson
1730	Edward Walpole	1809	Richard Wharton
1739	Stephen Fox	1814	Stephen Rumbold Lushington
1741	Henry Legge		
1742	Henry Furnese	1823	J.C.Herries
1742	John Jeffreys	1827	Thomas Frankland Lewis
1746	James West	1828	George Robert Dawson
1752	Nicholas Hardinge	1830	Thomas Spring Rice
1756	Samuel Martin	1834	Francis Thornhill Baring
1757	James West	1834	Sir Thomas Fremantle
1758	Samuel Martin	1835	Sir Francis Thornhill Baring
1762	Jeremiah Dyson		
1763	Charles Jenkinson	1839	Robert Gordon
1763	Thomas Whateley	1841	Richard More O'Ferrall
1765	Charles Lowndes	1841	Sir George Clerk
1765	Grey Cooper	1845	Edward Cardwell
1767	Thomas Bradshaw	1846	John Parker
1770	John Robinson	1849	William Goodenough Hayter
1782	Richard Burke	1850	Sir George Cornewall Lewis
1782	George Rose		
1783	Richard Brinsley Sheridan	1852	George Alexander Hamilton
1783	Thomas Steele	1853	James Wilson
1791	Charles Long	1858	George Alexander Hamilton
1801	Nicholas Vansittart	1859	Sir Stafford Northcote

1859	Samuel Laing	1916	Thomas McKinnon Wood
1860	Frederick Peel	1916-19	Sir Hardman Lever
1865	H.C.E.Childers	1917-21	Stanley Baldwin
1866	George Ward Hunt	1921-2	Edward Hilton Young
1868	George Sclater-Booth	1922	John Waller Hills
1868	Acton Smee Ayrton	1923	Archibald Boyd-Carpenter
1869	James Stansfeld	1923	Sir William Joynson-Hicks
1871	William Edward Baxter	1923	Walter Guinness
1873	John George Dodson	1924	William Graham
1874	William Henry Smith	1924	Walter Guinness
1877	Frederick A.Stanley	1925	Ronald John McNeill
1878	Sir Henry Selwin-Ibbetson	1927	Arthur Samuel
1880	Lord Frederick Cavendish	1929	Frederick Pethick-Lawrence
1882	Leonard Henry Courtney		
1884	John Tomlinson Hibbert	1931	Walter Elliot
1885	Sir Henry Thurston Holland	1932	Leslie Hore-Belisha
		1934	Alfred Duff Cooper
1885	Sir Matthew White Ridley	1935	W.S.Morrison
1885	William Lawies Jackson	1936	John Colville
1886	Henry H.Fowler	1938	Euan Wallace
1886	William Lawies Jackson	1939	Harry Crookshank
1891	Sir John Eldon Gorst	1943	Ralph Assheton
1892	Sir John Tomlinson Hibbert	1944	Osbert Peake
1895	Robert William Hanbury	1945	William Glenvil Hall
1900	Austen Chamberlain	1950	Douglas Jay
1902	William Hayes Fisher	1951	John Boyd-Carpenter
1903	Arthur Elliott	1954	Henry Brooke
1903	Victor Cavendish	1957	Enoch Powell
1905	Reginald McKenna	1958	Jocelyn Simon
1907	Walter Runciman	1959	Sir Edward Boyle
1908	Charles Hobhouse	1962	Anthony Barber
1911	Thomas McKinnon Wood	1963	Alan Green
1912	C.F.G.Masterman	1964	Niall MacDermot
1914	Edwin Montagu	1967	Harold Lever
1915	Francis Dyke Acland	1969	Dick Taverne
1915	Edwin Montagu	1970	Patrick Jenkin

1972   Terence Higgins
1974   John Gilbert
1975   Robert Sheldon
1979   Nigel Lawson
1981   Nicholas Ridley

ECONOMIC SECRETARY TO THE TREASURY (1947-64)

1947	Douglas Jay	1958	Office vacant
1950	Office vacant	1958	Frederick Erroll
1950	John Edwards	1959	Anthony Barber
1952	Reginald Maudling	1962	Edward du Cann
1955	Sir Edward Boyle	1963	Maurice Macmillan
1956	Derek Walker-Smith	1964	Anthony Crosland
1957	Nigel Birch		

MINISTER OF STATE (from 1968)

1968	Dick Taverne	1979-	Lord Cockfield
1969	William Rodgers	1981-	Jock Bruce-Gardyne
1970	Terence Higgins		
1972	John Nott		
1974	Robert Sheldon		
1975	Denzil Davies		
1979-81	Peter Rees		

CHIEF SECRETARY TO THE TREASURY

1961	Henry Brooke	1974	Joel Barnett
1962	John Boyd-Carpenter	1979	John Biffen
1964	John Diamond	1981	Leon Brittan
1970	Maurice Macmillan		
1972	Patrick Jenkin		
1974	Thomas Boardman		

MINISTER FOR ECONOMIC AFFAIRS

1947-7	Sir Stafford Cripps	1951-2	Sir Arthur Salter
1950-50	Hugh Gaitskell		

SECRETARY OF STATE FOR ECONOMIC AFFAIRS (1964-9)

1964	George Brown	1967	Peter Shore
1966	Michael Stewart		

MINISTER OF STATE

1964	Anthony Crosland	1967	Office vacant
1965	Austen Albu	1968	Thomas Urwin

UNDER-SECRETARY

1964-6	Maurice Foley	1967-7	Peter Shore
1964-7	William Rodgers	1967-9	Alan Williams
1967-7	Harold Lever	1967-8	Edmund Dell

LORD CHANCELLOR

LORD CHANCELLOR AND KEEPER OF THE GREAT SEAL

1068	Herfast	1226	Ralph Neville
1070	Osmund	1238	William de Cantilupe
1078	Maurice	1240	Richard, Abbot of Evesham
1085	Gerard	1242	Ralph Neville
1092	Robert Bloet	1244	Silvester of Everdon
1093	William Giffard	1246	John Mansel
1101	Roger, Bishop of Salisbury	1249	John Lexington
1102	Waldric	1250	William de Kilkenny
1107	Ranulf	1255	Henry Wingham
1123	Geoffrey Rufus	1258	Walter de Merton
1133	Robert de Sigillo	1260	Nicholas of Ely
1135	Roger le Poer	1263	John Chishull
1139	Philip de Harcourt	1264	Thomas Cantilupe
1140	Robert de Gant	1265	Walter Gifford
1154	Thomas Becket	1266	Godfrey Gifford
1162	Geoffrey Ridel	1268	John Chishull
1173	Ralph de Warneville	1269	Richard Middleton
1182	Geoffrey Plantagenet	1272	Walter de Merton
1189	William Longchamp	1274	Robert Burnell
1197	Eustace, Bishop of Ely	1292	John Langton
1199	Hubert Walter	1302	William Greenfield
1205	Walter de Grey	1304	William Hamilton
1214	Richard Marsh	1307	Ralph Baldock

1310	Walter Reynolds	1399	John Scarle
1314	John Sandale	1401	Edmund Stafford
1318	John Hotham	1403	Henry Beaufort
1320	John Salmon	1405	Thomas Langley
1323	Robert Baldock	1407	Thomas Arundel
1327	John Hotham	1410	Thomas Beaufort
1327	Henry Burghersh	1412	Thomas Arundel
1330	John Stratford	1413	Henry Beaufort
1334	Richard de Bury	1417	Thomas Langley
1335	John Stratford	1424	Henry Beaufort
1337	Robert Stratford	1426	John Kemp
1338	Richard Bintworth	1432	John Stafford
1340	John Stratford	1450	John Kemp
1340	Robert Stratford	1454	Earl of Salisbury
1340	Sir Robert Bourchier	1455	Thomas Bourchier
1341	Sir Robert Parving	1456	William Waynflete
1343	Sir Robert Sadington	1460	George Neville
1345	John Offord	1467	Robert Stillington
1349	John Thoresby	1470	George Neville
1356	William Edington	1471	Robert Stillington
1363	Simon Langham	1473	Laurence Booth
1367	William of Wykeham	1474	Thomas Rotherham
1371	Sir Robert Thorpe	1475	John Alcock
1372	Sir John Knyvett	1475	Thomas Rotherham
1377	Adam Houghton	1483	John Russell
1378	Richard Scrope	1485	Thomas Rotherham
1379	Simon Sudbury	1485	John Alcock
1381	William Courtenay	1486	John Morton
1381	Richard Scrope	1500	Henry Deane
1382	Robert Braybrook	1502	William Warham
1383	Sir Michael de la Pole	1515	Thomas Wolsey
1386	Thomas Arundel	1529	Sir Thomas More
1389	William of Wykeham	1532	Sir Thomas Audley
1391	Thomas Arundel	1544	Lord Wriothesley
1396	Edmund Stafford	1547	Lord St John
1399	Thomas Arundel	1547	Lord Rich

1551	Thomas Goodrich	1718	Lord Macclesfield
1553	Stephen Gardiner	1725	Lord King
1555	In commission	1733	Lord Talbot of Hensol
1556	Nicholas Heath	1737	Earl of Hardwicke
1558	Sir Nicholas Bacon	1757	Sir Robert Henley (the last Lord Keeper)
1579	Sir Thomas Bromley		
1587	Sir Christopher Hatton	1766	Lord Camden
1591	In commission	1770	Charles Yorke
1592	Sir John Puckering	1770	In commission
1596	Sir Thomas Egerton, Lord Ellesmere	1771	Lord Apsley
		1778	Lord Thurlow
1617	Sir Francis Bacon	1783	In commission
1621	John Williams	1783	Lord Thurlow
1625	Sir Thomas Coventry	1792	In commission
1640	Sir John Finch	1793	Lord Loughborough
1641	Sir Edward Littleton	1801	Lord Eldon
1645	Sir Richard Lane	1806	Lord Erskine
1649–1660	In commission under the Commonwealth	1807	Lord Eldon
		1827	Lord Lyndhurst
1653	Sir Edward Herbert, appointed by Charles II in exile	1830	Lord Brougham
		1834	Lord Lyndhurst
1658	Sir Edward Hyde, appointed by Charles II in exile	1836	Lord Cottenham
		1841	Lord Lyndhurst
1660	Sir Edward Hyde	1846	Lord Cottenham
1667	Sir Orlando Bridgeman	1850	Lord Truro
1672	Earl of Shaftesbury	1852	Lord St Leonards
1672	Sir Heneage Finch	1852	Lord Cranworth
1682	Sir Francis North	1858	Lord Chelmsford
1685	Lord Jeffreys	1859	Lord Campbell
1689–93	Great Seal in commission	1861	Lord Westbury
		1865	Lord Cranworth
1693	Sir John Somers	1866	Lord Chelmsford
1700	Sir Nathan Wright	1868	Lord Cairns
1705	William Cowper	1868	Lord Hatherley
1710	Sir Simon Harcourt	1872	Lord Selborne
1714	Lord (formerly William) Cowper	1874	Earl (formerly Lord) Cairns

1880	Earl of (formerly Lord) Selborne	1935	Viscount (formerly Lord) Hailsham (First Viscount)
1885	Lord Halsbury	1938	Lord Maugham
1886	Lord Herschell	1939	Viscount Caldecote
1886	Lord Halsbury	1940	Viscount Simon
1892	Lord Herschell	1945	Lord Jowitt
1895	Earl of (formerly Lord) Halsbury	1951	Lord Simonds
		1954	Viscount Kilmuir
1905	Lord Loreburn	1962	Lord Dilhorne
1912	Viscount Haldane	1964	Lord Gardiner
1915	Lord Buckmaster	1970	Lord Hailsham (formerly Second Viscount)
1916	Lord Finlay		
1919	Lord Birkenhead	1974	Lord Elwyn-Jones
1922	Viscount Cave	1979	Lord Hailsham
1924	Viscount Haldane		
1924	Viscount Cave		
1928	Lord Hailsham		
1929	Lord Sankey		

LORD PRESIDENT OF THE COUNCIL

LORD PRESIDENT OF THE COUNCIL

1679	Earl of Shaftesbury	1721	Lord Carleton
1679	Earl of Radnor	1725	Duke of Devonshire
1684	Earl of Rochester	1730	Lord Trevor
1685	Marquess of Halifax	1730	Earl of Wilmington
1685	Earl of Sunderland (Second Earl)	1742	Earl of Harrington
		1745	Duke of Dorset
1689	Earl of Danby	1751	Earl Granville
1699	Earl of Pembroke and Montgomery	1763	Duke of Bedford
		1765	Earl of Winchilsea and Nottingham
1701	Duke of Somerset		
1702	Earl of Pembroke and Montgomery	1766	Earl of Northington
		1767	Earl Gower
1708	Lord Somers	1779	Earl Bathurst
1710	Earl of Rochester	1782	Lord Camden
1711	Duke of Buckingham and Normanby	1783	Viscount Stormont
		1783	Earl Gower
1714	Earl of Nottingham	1784	Lord Camden
1715	Earl of Dorset	1794	Earl Fitzwilliam
1716	Duke of Devonshire	1794	Earl of Mansfield
1717	Earl of Sunderland (Third Earl)	1796	Earl of Chatham
		1801	Duke of Portland (Third Duke)
1719	Duke of Kingston		
1720	Viscount Townshend	1805	Viscount Sidmouth

1805	Earl (formerly Lord) Camden	1905	Earl of Crewe
		1908	Lord Tweedmouth
1806	Earl Fitzwilliam	1908	Viscount Wolverhampton
1806	Viscount Sidmouth	1910	Earl Beauchamp
1807	Earl Camden	1910	Viscount Morley
1812	Viscount Sidmouth	1914	Earl Beauchamp
1812	Earl of Harrowby	1915	Marquess (formerly Earl) of Crewe
1827	Duke of Portland (Fourth Duke)		
		1916	Earl Curzon
1828	Earl Bathurst	1919	Arthur Balfour
1830	Marquess of Lansdowne	1922	Marquess of Salisbury (Fourth Marquess)
1834	Earl of Rosslyn		
1835	Marquess of Lansdowne	1924	Lord Parmoor
1841	Lord Wharncliffe	1924	Marquess (formerly Earl) Curzon
1846	Duke of Buccleuch		
1846	Marquess of Lansdowne	1925	Earl of (formerly Arthur) Balfour
1852	Earl of Lonsdale		
1854	Lord John Russell	1929	Lord Parmoor
1855	Earl Granville	1931	Stanley Baldwin
1858	Marquess of Salisbury	1935	James Ramsay MacDonald
1859	Earl Granville	1937	Viscount Halifax
1866	Duke of Buckingham and Chandos	1938	Viscount Hailsham (First Viscount)
1867	Duke of Marlborough	1938	Viscount Runciman
1868	Earl de Grey and Ripon	1939	Earl Stanhope
1873	Henry Austin Bruce	1940	Neville Chamberlain
1874	Duke of Richmond	1940	Sir John Anderson
1880	Earl Spencer	1943	Clement Attlee
1883	Lord Carlingford	1945	Lord Woolton
1885	Viscount Cranbrook	1945	Herbert Morrison
1886	Earl Spencer	1951	Viscount Addison
1886	Viscount Cranbrook	1951	Lord Woolton
1892	Earl of Kimberley	1952	Marquess of Salisbury (Fifth Marquess)
1894	Earl of Rosebery		
1895	Duke of Devonshire	1957	Earl of Home
1903	Marquess of Londonderry	1957	Viscount Hailsham (Second Viscount)

19   Lord President of the Council

1959	Earl of Home	1974	Edward Short
1960	Viscount Hailsham (Second Viscount)	1976	Michael Foot
		1979	Lord Soames
1964	Herbert Bowden	1981	Francis Pym
1966	Richard Crossman		
1968	Frederick Peart		
1970	William Whitelaw		
1972	Robert Carr		
1972	James Prior		

MINISTER OF STATE, PRIVY COUNCIL OFFICE (1974-9)

1974	Gerald Fowler	1976	John Smith
1976	Lord Crowther-Hunt	1979	Lady Birk

PARLIAMENTARY SECRETARY (1974-9)

1974   William Price

LORD PRIVY SEAL

1307	William Melton	1360	John Buckingham
1312	Roger Northburgh	1363	William of Wykeham
1316	Thomas Charlton	1367	Peter Lacy
1320	Robert Baldock	1371	Nicholas Carew
1323	Robert Wodehouse	1377	John Fordham
1323	Robert Ayleston	1381	William Dighton
1324	William Airmyn	1382	Walter Skirlaw
1325	Henry Cliff	1386	John Waltham
1325	William Herlaston	1389	Edmund Stafford
1326	Robert Wyvill	1396	Guy Mone
1327	Richard Airmyn	1397	Richard Clifford
1328	Adam Lymbergh	1401	Thomas Langley
1329	Richard Bury	1405	Nicholas Bubwith
1334	Robert Ayleston	1406	John Prophet
1334	Robert Tawton	1415	John Wakering
1335	William de la Zouche	1416	Henry Ware
1337	Richard Bintworth	1418	John Kemp
1338	William Kilsby	1421	John Stafford
1342	John Offord	1422	William Alnwick
1344	Thomas Hatfield	1432	William Lyndwood
1345	John Thoresby	1443	Thomas Beckington
1347	Simon Islip	1444	Adam Moleyns
1350	Michael Northburgh	1450	Andrew Holes
1354	Thomas Bramber	1452	Thomas Lisieux
1355	John Winwick	1456	Laurence Booth

1460	Robert Stillington	1685	In commission
1467	Thomas Rotherham	1687	Lord Arundel of Wardour
1470	John Hales	1689	Marquess of Halifax
1471	Thomas Rotherham	1690	In commission
1474	John Russell	1692	Earl of Pembroke
1483	John Gunthorp	1697	In commission
1485	Peter Courtenay	1699	Viscount Lonsdale
1487	Richard Fox	1700	Earl of Tankerville
1516	Thomas Routhall	1701	In commission
1523	Lord Marny	1702	Marquess of Normanby
1523	Cuthbert Tunstall	1705	Duke of Newcastle
1530	Earl of Wiltshire	1711	In commission
1536	Lord Cromwell	1713	Earl of Dartmouth
1540	Earl of Southampton	1714	Marquess of Wharton
1542	Lord Russell	1715	In commission
1555	Lord Paget	1715	Earl of Sunderland
1559	Lord Burghley	1716	In commission
1572	Lord Howard of Effingham	1716	Duke of Kingston
1573	Sir Thomas Smith	1719	Duke of Kent
1576	Francis Walsingham	1720	Duke of Kingston
1590	Lord Burghley	1726	Lord Trevor
1598	Sir Robert Cecil	1730	Earl of Wilmington
1608	Earl of Northampton	1731	In commission
1614	Earl of Somerset	1731	Duke of Devonshire
1616	Earl of Worcester	1733	Viscount Lonsdale
1628	Sir John Coke	1735	Earl of Godolphin
1628	Sir Robert Naunton	1740	Lord Hervey
1628	Earl of Manchester	1742	Lord Gower
1643	Sir Edward Nicholas	1743	Earl of Cholmondeley
1644	Earl of Bath	1744	Lord Gower
1655	Nathaniel Fiennes	1755	Duke of Marlborough
1661	Lord Robartes	1755	Earl Gower
1669	In commission	1757	Earl Temple
1673	Earl of Anglesey	1761	In commission
1682	Marquess of Halifax	1761	Duke of Bedford
1685	Earl of Clarendon	1763	Duke of Marlborough

1765	Duke of Newcastle	1842	Duke of Buccleuch
1766	Earl of Chatham	1846	Earl of Haddington
1768	In commission	1846	Earl of Minto
1768	Earl of Chatham	1852	Marquess of Salisbury
1768	Earl of Bristol	1853	Duke of Argyll
1770	Earl of Halifax	1855	Earl of Harrowby (Second Earl)
1771	Earl of Suffolk and Berkshire	1858	Marquess of Clanricarde
1771	Duke of Grafton	1858	Earl of Hardwicke
1775	Earl of Dartmouth	1859	Duke of Argyll
1782	Duke of Grafton	1866	Earl of Malmesbury
1783	Earl of Carlisle	1868	Earl of Kimberley
1783	Duke of Rutland	1870	Viscount Halifax
1784	In commission	1874	Earl of Malmesbury
1784	Earl Gower	1876	Benjamin Disraeli
1794	In commission	1878	Duke of Northumberland
1794	Duke of Marlborough	1880	Duke of Argyll
1794	Earl of Chatham (Second Earl)	1881	Lord Carlingford
		1885	Earl of Rosebery
1798	Earl of Westmorland	1885	Earl of Harrowby (Third Earl)
1806	Viscount Sidmouth		
1807	Lord Holland	1886	William Ewart Gladstone
1807	Earl of Westmorland	1886	Earl Cadogan
1827	Duke of Devonshire	1892	William Ewart Gladstone
1827	Earl of Carlisle	1894	Lord Tweedmouth
1828	Lord Ellenborough	1895	Viscount Cross
1829	Earl of Rosslyn	1900	Marquess of Salisbury (Third Marquess)
1830	Lord Durham		
1833	Earl of Ripon	1902	Arthur Balfour
1834	Earl of Carlisle	1903	Marquess of Salisbury (Fourth Marquess)
1834	Earl of Mulgrave		
1834	Lord Wharncliffe	1905	Marquess of Ripon
1835	Viscount Duncannon	1908	Earl of Crewe
1840	Earl of Clarendon	1911	Earl Carrington
1841	Duke of Buckingham and Chandos	1912	Marquess (formerly Earl) of Crewe

1915	Earl Curzon
1916	Earl of Crawford
1919	Andrew Bonar Law
1921	Austen Chamberlain
1922	Office vacant
1923	Lord Robert Cecil
1924	J.R.Clynes
1924	Marquess of Salisbury (Fourth Marquess)
1929	J.H.Thomas
1930	Vernon Hartshorn
1931	Thomas Johnston
1931	Earl Peel
1931	Viscount Snowden
1932	Stanley Baldwin
1933	Anthony Eden
1935	Marquess of Londonderry
1935	Viscount Halifax
1937	Earl De La Warr
1938	Sir John Anderson
1939	Sir Samuel Hoare
1940	Sir Kingsley Wood
1940	Clement Attlee
1942	Sir Stafford Cripps
1942	Viscount Cranborne
1943	Lord Beaverbrook
1945	Arthur Greenwood
1947	Lord Inman
1947	Viscount Addison
1951	Ernest Bevin
1951	Richard Stokes
1951	Marquess of Salisbury (Fifth Marquess, formerly Viscount Cranborne)
1952	Harry Crookshank
1955	R.A.Butler
1959	Viscount Hailsham
1960	Edward Heath
1963	Selwyn Lloyd
1964	Earl of Longford
1965	Sir Frank Soskice
1966	Earl of Longford
1968	Lord Shackleton
1968	Frederick Peart
1968	Lord Shackleton
1970	Earl Jellicoe
1973	Lord Windlesham
1974	Lord Shepherd
1976	Lord (formerly Frederick) Peart
1979	Sir Ian Gilmour
1981	Humphrey Atkins

CHANCELLOR OF THE DUCHY OF LANCASTER

1399	William Burgoyne		1568	Sir Ralph Sadler
1399	John Wakering		1587	Sir Francis Walsingham
1405	Thomas Stanley		1590	Sir Thomas Heneage
1410	John Springthorpe		1595	In commission
1413	John Wodehouse		1597	Sir Robert Cecil
1431	Walter Sherington		1599	In commission
1442	William Tresham		1601	Sir John Fortescue
1449	John Say		1607	Sir John Fortescue and Sir Thomas Parry
1471	Sir Richard Fowler			
1477	Sir John Say		1615	Sir Thomas Parry and John Daccombe
1478	Thomas Thwaites			
1483	Thomas Metcalfe		1616	Sir John Daccombe
1485	Sir Reginald Bray		1618	Sir Humphrey May
1504	Sir John Mordaunt		1629	Lord Newburgh
1505	Sir Richard Empson		1645	Lord Grey of Werke and William Lenthall
1509	Sir Henry Marney			
1523	Sir Richard Wingfield		1648	Sir Gilbert Gerard
1525	Sir Thomas More		1649	John Bradshawe
1529	Sir William Fitzwilliam		1655	Thomas Fell
1533	Sir John Gage		1658	John Bradshawe
1547	Sir William Paget		1660	William Lenthall
1552	Sir John Gates		1660	Lord Seymour
1553	Sir Robert Rochester		1664	Sir Thomas Ingram
1558	Sir Edward Walgrave		1672	Sir Robert Carr
1558	Sir Ambrose Cave		1682	Sir Thomas Chicheley

1687	In commission	1840	Earl of Clarendon
1687	Robert Phelipps	1841	Sir George Grey
1689	Lord Willoughby d'Eresby	1841	Lord Granville Somerset
1697	Earl of Stamford	1846	Lord Campbell
1702	Sir John Leveson Gower	1850	Earl of Carlisle
1706	Earl of Derby	1852	Robert Adam Christopher
1710	Lord Berkeley of Stratton	1852	Edward Strutt
1714	Earl of Aylesford	1854	Earl Granville
1716	Earl of Scarborough	1855	Earl of Harrowby
1717	Nicholas Lechmere	1855	Matthew Talbot Baines
1727	Duke of Rutland	1858	Duke of Montrose
1735	Earl of Cholmondeley	1859	Sir George Grey
1743	Lord Mount Edgcumbe	1861	Edward Cardwell
1758	Viscount Dupplin, Earl of Kinnoull	1864	Earl of Clarendon
		1866	George J.Goschen
1762	Lord Strange	1866	Earl of Devon
1771	Lord Hyde, Earl of Clarendon	1867	John Wilson Patten
		1868	Thomas Edward Taylor
1782	Lord Ashburton	1868	Frederick Temple, Earl Dufferin
1783	Earl of Derby		
1783	Earl of Clarendon	1872	H.C.E.Childers
1786	Lord Hawkesbury	1873	John Bright
1803	Lord Pelham	1874	Thomas Edward Taylor
1804	Lord Mulgrave	1880	John Bright
1805	Earl of Buckinghamshire	1882	Earl of Kimberley
1805	Lord Harrowby	1882	John George Dodson
1806	Earl of Derby	1884	G.O.Trevelyan
1807	Spencer Perceval	1885	Henry Chaplin
1812	Earl of Buckinghamshire	1886	Edward Heneage
1812	Charles Bathurst	1886	Sir Ughtred James Kay-Shuttleworth
1823	Lord Bexley		
1828	Earl of Aberdeen	1886	Viscount Cranbrook
1828	Charles Arbuthnot	1886	Lord John Manners, Duke of Rutland
1830	Lord Holland		
1834	C.W.Williams Wynn	1892	James Bryce
1834	Lord Holland	1894	Lord Tweedmouth

1895	Viscount Cross	1940	George Tryon
1895	Lord James of Hereford	1940	Lord Hankey
1902	Sir William Hood Walrond	1941	Alfred Duff Cooper
1905	Sir Henry H.Fowler	1943	Ernest Brown
1908	Lord Fitzmaurice	1945	Sir Arthur Salter
1909	Herbert Samuel	1945	John Hynd
1910	Joseph Pease	1947	Lord Pakenham
1911	Charles Hobhouse	1948	Hugh Dalton
1914	C.F.G.Masterman	1950	Viscount Alexander
1915	Edwin Montagu	1951	Viscount Swinton
1915	Winston Churchill	1952	Lord Woolton
1915	Herbert Samuel	1955	Earl of Selkirk
1916	Edwin Montagu	1957	Charles Hill
1916	Thomas McKinnon Wood	1961	Iain Macleod
1916	Sir Frederick Cawley	1963	Lord Blakenham
1918	Lord Beaverbrook	1964	Douglas Houghton
1918	Lord Downham	1966	George Thomson
1919	Earl of Crawford	1967	Frederick Lee
1921	Viscount Peel	1969	George Thomson
1922	Sir William Sutherland	1970	Anthony Barber
1922	Marquess of Salisbury	1970	Geoffrey Rippon
1923	J.C.C.Davidson	1972	John Davies
1924	Josiah Wedgwood	1974	Harold Lever
1924	Viscount Cecil	1979	Norman St John-Stevas
1927	Lord Cushendun	1981	Francis Pym
1929	Sir Oswald Mosley	1981	Lady Young
1930	Clement Attlee		
1931	Lord Ponsonby		
1931	Marquess of Lothian		
1931	J.C.C.Davidson		
1937	Earl Winterton		
1939	W.S.Morrison		

PAYMASTER-GENERAL

1836	Sir Henry Parnell	1880	Lord Wolverton
1841	Edward John Stanley	1885	Earl Beauchamp
1841	Sir Edward Knatchbull	1886	Lord Thurlow
1845	William Bingham Baring	1886	Earl Beauchamp
1846	Thomas Babington Macaulay	1887	Earl Brownlow
1848	Earl Granville	1890	Earl of Jersey
1852	Lord Stanley of Alderley (formerly E.J.Stanley)	1891	Lord Windsor
		1892	Charles Seale-Hayne
1852	Lord Colchester	1895	Earl of Hopetoun
1853	Lord Stanley of Alderley	1899	Duke of Marlborough
1855	Edward Pleydell Bouverie	1902	Sir Savile Brinton Crossley
1855	Robert Lowe		
1858	Earl of Donoughmore	1905	Richard Causton
1859	Lord Lovaine	1910	Ivor Guest
1859	James Wilson	1912	Lord Strachie
1859	William Francis Cowper	1915	Lord Newton
1860	William Hutt	1916	Arthur Henderson
1865	George J.Goschen	1916	Sir Joseph Compton-Rickett
1866	William Monsell		
1866	Stephen Cave	1919	Sir Tudor Walters
1868	Lord Dufferin and Clandeboye	1922	Office vacant
		1923	Neville Chamberlain
1872	H.C.E.Childers	1923	Sir William Joynson-Hicks
1873	William Patrick Adam	1923	Archibald Boyd-Carpenter
1874	Stephen Cave	1924	Henry Gosling

1924	Office vacant	1955	Office vacant
1925	Duke of Sutherland	1956	Sir Walter Monckton
1928	Earl of Onslow	1957	Reginald Maudling
1929	Lord Arnold	1959	Lord Mills
1931	Office vacant	1961	Henry Brooke
1931	Sir Tudor Walters	1962	John Boyd-Carpenter
1931	Lord Rochester	1964	George Wigg
1935	Lord Hutchison	1967	Office vacant
1938	Earl of Munster	1968	Lord Shackleton
1939	Earl Winterton	1968	Judith Hart
1939	Office vacant	1969	Harold Lever
1940	Viscount Cranborne	1970	Viscount Eccles
1940	Office vacant	1973	Maurice Macmillan
1941	Lord Hankey	1974	Edmund Dell
1942	Sir William Jowitt	1976	Shirley Williams
1942	Lord Cherwell	1979	Angus Maude
1945	Office vacant	1981	Francis Pym
1946	Arthur Greenwood	1981	Cecil Parkinson
1947	Hilary Marquand		
1948	Viscount Addison		
1949	Lord Macdonald		
1951	Lord Cherwell		
1953	Earl of Selkirk		

SECRETARY OF STATE

SECRETARY OF STATE

1253	John Maunsell	1536	Thomas Wriothesley
1278	Francis Accursii	1539	Thomas Wriothesley and Sir Ralph Sadler
1299	John de Benstede		
1308	William de Melton	1543	Sir William Petre, vice Wriothesley
	-----	1543	Sir William Paget, vice Sadler
1379	Robert Braybrooke	1548	Sir William Petre and Sir Thomas Smith
1402	John Prophet		
1415	John Stone	1549	Nicholas Wotton and Sir William Petre
1421	William Alnwick		
1432	William Hayton	1549	Sir William Cecil, vice Wotton
1439	Thomas Beckington		
1460	Thomas Manning	1550	Sir William Petre and Sir William Cecil
1464	William Hatcliffe		
1480	Oliver King	1553	Sir John Cheke, in addition to above
1483	John Kendal		
1485	Richard Fox	1553	Sir William Petre and Sir John Bourne
1487	Oliver King		
1500	Thomas Routhall	1557	John Boxall
1516	Richard Pace	1558	Sir William Cecil, Lord Burleigh, alone
1526	William Knight		
1528	Stephen Gardiner	1572-6	Sir Thomas Smith
1533	Thomas Cromwell		

1577   Sir Francis Walsingham
       and Thomas Wilson

1581   Sir Francis Walsingham,
       alone

1586   Sir Francis Walsingham
       and William Davison

1587   Sir Francis Walsingham,
       alone

1590   Office vacant

1596   Sir Robert Cecil

1600   John Herbert

1612   Viscount Rochester

1614   Sir Ralph Winwood

1616   Sir Ralph Winwood and
       Sir Thomas Lake

1618   Sir John Herbert,
       vice Winwood

1618   Sir Robert Naunton,
       vice Herbert

1619   Sir George Calvert,
       vice Lake

1623   Sir Edward Conway,
       vice Naunton

1625   Sir Albertus Morton and
       Lord (formerly Sir
       Edward) Conway

1625   Sir John Coke,
       vice Morton

1628   Viscount Dorchester,
       vice Conway

1632   Sir Francis Windebanke,
       vice Dorchester

1640   Sir Harry Vane,
       vice Coke

1641   Sir Edward Nicholas,
       vice Windebanke

1642   Viscount Falkland,
       vice Vane

1643   Lord Digby,
       vice Falkland

From 1660 the office was divided into Northern and Southern
Departments.

Northern Department

1660   Sir William Morrice

1668   Sir John Trevor

1672   Henry Coventry

1674   Sir Joseph Williamson

1678   Earl of Sunderland
       (Second Earl)

1680   Sir Leoline Jenkins

1681   Earl of Conway

1683   Earl of Sunderland
       (Second Earl)

1684   Sidney Godolphin

1684   Earl of Middleton

1688   Viscount Preston

1689   Earl of Nottingham (Sole
       Secretary from June to
       December 1690)

1690   Viscount Sydney

1692   Earl of Nottingham (Sole
       Secretary)

1693 Sir John Trenchard (Sole Secretary from November 1693 to March 1694)

1694 Earl of Shrewsbury

1695 Sir William Trumbull

1697 James Vernon (Sole Secretary from December 1698 to May 1699)

1700 Sir Charles Hedges

1702 James Vernon

1702 Sir Charles Hedges

1704 Robert Harley

1710 Henry Boyle

1713 William Bromley

1714 Viscount Townshend

1716 James Stanhope

1717 Earl of Sunderland (Third Earl)

1718 Viscount (formerly James) Stanhope

1721 Viscount Townshend

1723 Robert Walpole (Sole Secretary)

1724 Viscount Townshend

1730 Lord Harrington

1742 Lord Carteret

1744 Earl of (formerly Lord) Harrington

1746 Earl of Chesterfield

1748 Duke of Newcastle

1754 Earl of Holdernesse

1761 Earl of Bute

1762 George Grenville

1762 Earl of Halifax

1763 Earl of Sandwich

1765 Duke of Grafton

1766 Henry Seymour Conway

1768 Viscount Weymouth

1768 Earl of Rochford

1770 Earl of Sandwich

1771 Earl of Halifax

1771 Earl of Suffolk and Berkshire

1779 Viscount Weymouth (Sole Secretary)

1779 Viscount Stormont

Southern Department

1659 Sir Edward Nicholas

1662 Sir Henry Bennet

1674 Henry Coventry

1679 Earl of Sunderland (Second Earl)

1681 Sir Leoline Jenkins

1684 Earl of Sunderland (Second Earl)

1688 Earl of Middleton

1689 Earl of Shrewsbury

1690 Earl of Nottingham (Sole Secretary from March 1692 to March 1693)

1693 Sir John Trenchard (Sole Secretary from November 1693 to March 1694)

1695	Earl of Shrewsbury	1723	Robert Walpole (Sole Secretary)
1698	James Vernon (Sole Secretary from December 1698 to May 1699)	1724	Lord Carteret
		1724	Duke of Newcastle
1699	Earl of Jersey	1748	Duke of Bedford
1700	James Vernon (Sole Secretary from June to November 1700)	1751	Earl of Holdernesse
		1754	Sir Thomas Robinson
		1755	Henry Fox
1702	Earl of Manchester	1756	William Pitt
1702	Earl of Nottingham	1761	Earl of Egremont
1704	Sir Charles Hedges	1763	Earl of Halifax
1706	Earl of Sunderland (Third Earl)	1765	Henry Seymour Conway
		1766	Duke of Richmond
1710	Lord Dartmouth	1766	Earl of Shelburne
1713	Henry St John	1768	Viscount Weymouth
1714	James Stanhope	1770	Earl of Rochford
1716	Paul Methuen	1775	Viscount Weymouth (Sole Secretary from March to October 1779)
1717	Joseph Addison		
1718	James Craggs		
1721	Lord Carteret	1779	Earl of Hillsborough

FIRST SECRETARY OF STATE (1962-70)

1962	R.A.Butler	1966	Michael Stewart
1963	Office vacant	1968	Barbara Castle
1964	George Brown		

HOME OFFICE

SECRETARY OF STATE FOR THE HOME DEPARTMENT

1782	Earl of Shelburne	1839	Marquess of Normanby
1782	Thomas Townshend	1841	Sir James Graham
1783	Lord North	1846	Sir George Grey
1783	Earl Temple	1852	Spencer Walpole
1783	Lord Sydney (formerly Thomas Townshend)	1852	Viscount Palmerston
		1855	Sir George Grey
1789	Lord Grenville	1858	Spencer Walpole
1791	Henry Dundas	1859	T.H.S.Sotheron-Estcourt
1794	Duke of Portland	1859	Sir George Cornewall Lewis
1801	Lord Pelham		
1803	Charles Yorke	1861	Sir George Grey
1804	Lord Hawkesbury	1866	Spencer Walpole
1806	Earl Spencer	1867	Gathorne Hardy
1807	Lord Hawkesbury	1868	Henry Austin Bruce
1809	Richard Ryder	1873	Robert Lowe
1812	Viscount Sidmouth	1874	Sir Richard Assheton Cross
1822	Robert Peel		
1827	William Sturges Bourne	1880	Sir William Harcourt
1827	Marquess of Lansdowne	1885	Sir Richard Assheton Cross
1828	Robert Peel		
1830	Viscount Melbourne	1886	H.C.E.Childers
1834	Viscount Duncannon	1886	Henry Matthews
1834	Henry Goulburn	1892	Herbert H.Asquith
1835	Lord John Russell	1895	Sir Matthew White Ridley

1900	C.T.Ritchie	1945	James Chuter Ede
1902	Aretas Akers-Douglas	1951	Sir David Maxwell Fyfe
1905	Herbert Gladstone	1954	Gwilym Lloyd-George
1910	Winston Churchill	1957	R.A.Butler
1911	Reginald McKenna	1962	Henry Brooke
1915	Sir John Simon	1964	Sir Frank Soskice
1916	Herbert Samuel	1966	Roy Jenkins
1916	Sir George Cave	1967	James Callaghan
1919	Edward Shortt	1970	Reginald Maudling
1922	William Bridgeman	1972	Robert Carr
1924	Arthur Henderson	1974	Roy Jenkins
1924	Sir William Joynson-Hicks	1976	Merlyn Rees
1929	J.R.Clynes	1979	William Whitelaw
1931	Sir Herbert Samuel		
1932	Sir John Gilmour		
1935	Sir John Simon		
1937	Sir Samuel Hoare		
1939	Sir John Anderson		
1940	Herbert Morrison		
1945	Sir Donald Somervell		

MINISTER OF STATE

1960	Denis Vosper	1974-6	Alexander Lyon
1961	David Renton	1976-9	Brynmor John
1962	Earl Jellicoe	1979-9	Lord Boston
1963	Lord Derwent	1979-81	Leon Brittan
1964	Alice Bacon	1979-	Timothy Raison
1967	Lord Stonham	1981-	Patrick Mayhew
1969	Shirley Williams		
1970-2	Richard Sharples		
1970-2	Lord Windlesham		
1972-4	Mark Carlisle		
1972-4	Viscount Colville		
1974-9	Lord Harris of Greenwich		

UNDER-SECRETARY OF STATE FOR THE HOME DEPARTMENT

1782	Edward Nepean	1852	Sir William George Hylton Jolliffe
1782	Thomas Orde		
1782	Henry Strachey	1853	Henry Fitzroy
1783	George Augustus North	1855	William Nathaniel Massey
1784	John Thomas Townshend	1858	Gathorne Hardy
1789	Scrope Bernard	1859	George Clive
1794	Thomas Brodrick	1863	Henry Austin Bruce
1796	Charles Greville	1864	Thomas George Baring
1798	William Wickham	1866	Edward H.Knatchbull-Hugessen
1801	Edward Finch Hatton		
1801	Sir George Shee	1866	Earl of Belmore
1803	Reginald Pole Carew	1867	Sir James Fergusson
1804	John Henry Smyth	1868	Sir Michael Hicks-Beach
1806	C.W.Willams Wynn	1868	Edward H.Knatchbull-Hugessen
1807	Cecil Jenkinson		
1810	Henry Goulburn	1871	H.S.P.Winterbotham
1812	John Hiley Addington	1874	Sir Henry John Selwin-Ibbetson
1818	Henry Clive		
1822	George Robert Dawson	1878	Sir Matthew White Ridley
1827	Spencer Perceval	1880	Leonard Henry Courtney
1827	Thomas Spring Rice	1881	Earl of Rosebery
1828	William Yates Peel	1883	John Tomlinson Hibbert
1830	Sir George Clerk	1884	Henry H.Fowler
1830	George Lamb	1885	Charles Beilby Stuart-Wortley
1834	Viscount Howick		
1834	Edward John Stanley	1886	Henry Broadhurst
1835	William Gregson	1886	Charles Beilby Stuart-Wortley
1835	Fox Maule		
1841	Lord Seymour	1892	Herbert Gladstone
1841	J.H.T.Manners Sutton	1894	G.W.E.Russell
1842	Sir William Marcus Somerville	1895	Jesse Collings
		1902	Thomas Cochrane
1847	Sir Denis Le Marchant	1905	Herbert Samuel
1848	George Cornewall Lewis	1909	C.F.G.Masterman
1850	Edward Pleydell Bouverie	1912	Ellis Jones Ellis-Griffith

1915	Cecil Harmsworth	1957-9	Patricia Hornsby-Smith
1915	William Brace	1957-8	Jocelyn Simon
1919	Sir Hamar Greenwood	1958-61	David Renton
1919	Sir John Laurence Baird	1959-60	Denis Vosper
1922	George F.Stanley	1961-2	Earl Bathurst
1923	Godfrey Locker-Lampson	1961-3	Charles Fletcher-Cooke
1924	Rhys Davies	1962-4	Christopher Woodhouse
1924	Godfrey Locker-Lampson	1963-4	Mervyn Pike
1925	Douglas Hewitt Hacking	1964-7	Lord Stonham
1927	Sir Vivian Henderson	1964-6	George Thomas
1929	Alfred Short	1966-7	Maurice Foley
1931	Oliver Stanley	1966-8	Dick Taverne
1933	Douglas Hewitt Hacking	1967-8	David Ennals
1934	Harry Crookshank	1968-70	Elystan Morgan
1935	Euan Wallace	1968-70	Merlyn Rees
1935	Geoffrey Lloyd	1970	Mark Carlisle
1939	Osbert Peake	1972	David Lane
1944	Earl of Munster	1974	Shirley Summerskill
1945	George Oliver	1979	Lord Belstead
1947	Kenneth Younger		
1950	Geoffrey de Freitas		
1951-2	David Llewellyn		
1952-5	Sir Hugh Lucas-Tooth		
1952-4	Lord Lloyd		
1954-7	Lord Mancroft		
1955-7	William Deedes		

PARLIAMENTARY SECRETARY TO THE MINISTRY OF HOME SECURITY (1939-45)

The Home Secretary also held the post of Minister of Home Security.

1939	Alan Lennox-Boyd	1940-5	Ellen Wilkinson
1939-42	William Mabane		

FOREIGN OFFICE AND OVERSEAS DEPARTMENTS

SECRETARY OF STATE FOR FOREIGN AFFAIRS (FOREIGN AND COMMONWEALTH AFFAIRS FROM 1968)

1782	Charles James Fox	1852	Earl of Malmesbury
1782	Lord Grantham	1852	Lord John Russell
1783	Charles James Fox	1853	Earl of Clarendon
1783	Marquess of Carmarthen	1858	Earl of Malmesbury
1791	Lord Grenville	1859	Lord John Russell
1801	Lord Hawkesbury	1865	Earl of Clarendon
1804	Lord Harrowby	1866	Lord Stanley
1805	Lord Mulgrave	1868	Earl of Clarendon
1806	Charles James Fox	1870	Earl Granville
1806	Lord Howick	1874	Earl of Derby (formerly Lord Stanley)
1807	George Canning		
1809	Earl Bathurst	1878	Marquess of Salisbury
1809	Marquess Wellesley	1880	Earl Granville
1812	Viscount Castlereagh	1885	Marquess of Salisbury
1822	George Canning	1886	Earl of Rosebery
1827	Earl of Dudley	1886	Earl of Iddesleigh
1828	Earl of Aberdeen	1887	Marquess of Salisbury
1830	Viscount Palmerston	1892	Earl of Rosebery
1834	Duke of Wellington	1894	Earl of Kimberley
1835	Viscount Palmerston	1895	Marquess of Salisbury
1841	Earl of Aberdeen	1900	Marquess of Lansdowne
1846	Viscount Palmerston	1905	Sir Edward Grey
1851	Earl Granville	1916	Arthur Balfour

1919	Earl Curzon	1964	Patrick Gordon Walker
1924	James Ramsay MacDonald	1965	Michael Stewart
1924	Austen Chamberlain	1966	George Brown
1929	Arthur Henderson	1968	Michael Stewart
1931	Marquess of Reading	1970	Sir Alec Douglas-Home (formerly Earl of Home)
1931	Sir John Simon		
1935	Sir Samuel Hoare	1974	James Callaghan
1935	Anthony Eden	1976	Anthony Crosland
1938	Viscount Halifax	1977	David Owen
1940	Anthony Eden	1979	Lord Carrington
1945	Ernest Bevin		
1951	Herbert Morrison		
1951	Sir Anthony Eden		
1955	Harold Macmillan		
1955	Selwyn Lloyd		
1960	Earl of Home		
1963	R.A.Butler		

MINISTER OF STATE

1943	Richard Law	1964-6	George Thomson
1945	William Mabane	1964-7	Walter Padley
1945	Philip Noel-Baker	1964-70	Lord Chalfont
1946	Hector McNeil	1966-7	Eirene White
1950	Kenneth Younger	1967-7	George Thomson
1951-4	Selwyn Lloyd	1967-9	Frederick Mulley
1953-7	Marquess of Reading	1967-9	Goronwy Roberts
1954-6	Anthony Nutting	1968-70	Lord Shepherd
1956-9	Allan Noble	1970-2	Joseph Godber
1957-61	David Ormsby-Gore	1972-4	Lady Tweedsmuir
1959-60	John Profumo	1972-4	Julian Amery
1961-3	Joseph Godber	1972-4	Lord Balniel
1961-4	Earl of Dundee	1974-6	David Ennals
1963-4	Peter Thomas	1974-6	Roy Hattersley
1964-70	Lord Caradon	1975-9	Lord Goronwy-Roberts

1976-7	David Owen	1979-	Neil Marten
1976-9	Edward Rowlands	1981-	Richard Luce
1977-9	Frank Judd		
1979-	Douglas Hurd		
1979-81	Nicholas Ridley		
1979-81	Peter Blaker		

UNDER-SECRETARY OF STATE FOR FOREIGN AFFAIRS

1782	Richard Brinsley Sheridan and William Fraser	1824	Lord Howard de Walden, additionally
1782	George Maddison, vice Sheridan	1826	Marquess of Clanricarde, vice Conyngham
1783	St Andrew St John, vice Maddison	1827	Lord Howard de Walden, alone
1783	William Fraser, alone	1828	Lord Dunglass
1789	James Bland Burgess, vice Fraser	1830	Sir George Shee
		1834	Viscount Fordwich
1789	Dudley Ryder, additionally	1834	Viscount Mahon
		1835	William Fox Strangways
1790	James Bland Burgess, alone	1840	Viscount Leveson
1796	George Canning	1841	Viscount Canning
1799	John Hookham Frere	1846	George A.F.P.S.Smythe
1800	Edward Fisher	1846	Edward John Stanley
1801	Lord Hervey	1852	Austen Henry Layard
1803	Charles Arbuthnot	1852	Edward Henry Stanley
1804	William Eliot	1852	Lord Wodehouse
1805	Robert Ward	1856	Earl of Shelburne
1806	George Walpole Sir Francis Vincent) jointly		
		1858	William Vesey Fitzgerald
1807	Viscount FitzHarris	1859	Lord Wodehouse
1807	Charles Bagot	1861	Austen Henry Layard
1809	Culling Charles Smith	1866	Edward Christopher Egerton
1812	Edward Cooke		
1822	Earl of Clanwilliam	1868	Arthur John Otway
1823	Lord Francis Conyngham	1871	Viscount Enfield

1874	Robert Bourke	1945-6	Hector McNeil
1880	Sir Charles Wentworth Dilke	1946-50	Christopher Mayhew
		1948-51	Lord Henderson
1883	Lord Edmond Fitzmaurice	1950-1	Ernest Davies
1885	Robert Bourke	1951-3	Marquess of Reading
1886	James Bryce	1951-4	Anthony Nutting
1886	Sir James Fergusson	1953-4	Douglas Dodds-Parker
1891	J.W.Lowther	1954-5	Robert Turton
1892	Sir Edward Grey	1954-6	Lord John Hope
1895	George Nathaniel Curzon	1955-7	Douglas Dodds-Parker
1898	St John Brodrick	1956-7	David Ormsby-Gore
1900	Viscount Cranborne	1957-8	Earl of Gosford
1903	Earl Percy	1957-8	Ian Harvey
1905	Lord Edmond Fitzmaurice (Lord Fitzmaurice)	1958-62	Marquess of Lansdowne
		1958-9	John Profumo
1908	Thomas McKinnon Wood	1959-60	Robert Allan
1911	Francis Dyke Acland	1960-1	Joseph Godber
1915	Neil Primrose	1961-3	Peter Thomas
1915	Lord Robert Cecil	1962-4	Peter Smithers
1919	Cecil Harmsworth	1964-4	Robert Mathew
1922	Ronald McNeill	1964-7	Lord Walston
1924	Arthur Ponsonby	1967-8	William Rodgers
1924	Ronald McNeill	1968-70	Maurice Foley
1925	Godfrey Locker-Lampson	1968-9	William Whitlock
1929	Hugh Dalton	1969-70	Evan Luard
1931	Anthony Eden	1970-3	Marquess of Lothian
1934-6	Earl Stanhope	1970-4	Anthony Royle
1935-8	Viscount Cranborne (for League of Nations Affairs)	1970-3	Anthony Kershaw
		1974-4	Peter Blaker
		1974-5	Lord Goronwy-Roberts
1936-9	Earl of Plymouth	1974-5	Joan Lestor
1938-41	R.A.Butler	1975-6	Edward Rowlands
1941	Richard Law	1976-9	Evan Luard
1943	George Hall	1976-9	John Tomlinson
1945-5	Lord Dunglass	1979-81	Richard Luce
1945-5	Lord Lovat	1981-	Lord Tregfarne

ASSISTANT UNDER-SECRETARY

1916-19 Lord Newton

SECRETARY OF STATE FOR THE COLONIES

1768	Earl of Hillsborough	1775	Lord George Germain
1772	Earl of Dartmouth	1782	Welbore Ellis

Post abolished in 1782 and duties transferred to Home Secretary until 1801. From 1801 to 1854 there was a post of Secretary of State for War and the Colonies, when the posts were again divided.

1854	Sir George Grey	1882	Earl of Derby (formerly Lord Stanley)
1855	Sidney Herbert		
1855	Lord John Russell	1885	Frederick A. Stanley
1855	Sir William Molesworth	1886	Earl Granville
1855	Henry Labouchere	1886	Edward Stanhope
1858	Lord Stanley	1887	Lord Knutsford
1858	Sir Edward Bulwer Lytton	1892	Marquess of Ripon
1859	Duke of Newcastle	1895	Joseph Chamberlain
1864	Edward Cardwell	1903	Alfred Lyttelton
1866	Earl of Carnarvon	1905	Earl of Elgin
1867	Duke of Buckingham and Chandos	1908	Earl of Crewe
		1910	Lewis Harcourt
1868	Earl Granville	1915	Andrew Bonar Law
1870	Earl of Kimberley	1916	Walter Long
1874	Earl of Carnarvon	1919	Viscount Milner
1878	Sir Michael Hicks-Beach	1921	Winston Churchill
1880	Earl of Kimberley	1922	Duke of Devonshire

1924	J.H.Thomas	1942	Oliver Stanley
1924	L.S.Amery	1945	George Hall
1929	Lord Passfield	1946	Arthur Creech Jones
1931	J.H.Thomas	1950	James Griffiths
1931	Sir Philip Cunliffe-Lister	1951	Oliver Lyttelton
1935	Malcolm MacDonald	1954	Alan Lennox-Boyd
1935	J.H.Thomas	1959	Iain Macleod
1936	William Ormsby-Gore	1961	Reginald Maudling
1938	Malcolm MacDonald	1962	Duncan Sandys
1940	Lord Lloyd	1964	Anthony Greenwood
1941	Lord Moyne	1965	Earl of Longford
1942	Viscount Cranborne	1966	Frederick Lee

The office became part of Commonwealth Affairs in 1966 and was abolished in 1967.

MINISTER OF STATE

1948	Earl of Listowel	1955	John Hare
1950	John Dugdale	1956	John Maclay
1951	Alan Lennox-Boyd	1957	Earl of Perth
1952	Henry Hopkinson	1962	Marquess of Lansdowne

UNDER-SECRETARY

1768	Richard Philips		---
1768	John Pownall, additionally		
		1854	Frederick Peel
1772	William Knox, vice Philips	1855	John Ball
		1857	Chichester Samuel Fortescue
1776	Christian D'Oyly, vice Pownall		
		1858	Earl of Carnarvon
1778	Thomas De Grey, vice D'Oyly	1859	Chichester Samuel Fortescue
1780	Benjamin Thomson, vice De Grey	1865	William Edward Forster

1866	Charles Bowyer Adderley	1922	William Ormsby-Gore
1868	William Monsell	1924	Lord Arnold
1871	Edward H.Knatchbull-Hugessen	1924	William Ormsby-Gore
		1929	William Lunn
1874	James Lowther	1929	Drummond Shiels
1878	Earl Cadogan	1931	Sir Robert Hamilton
1880	Mountstuart Elphinstone Grant-Duff	1932	Earl of Plymouth
		1936	Earl De La Warr
1881	Leonard Henry Courtney	1937	Marquess of Dufferin and Ava
1882	Anthony E.M.Ashley		
1885	Earl of Dunraven	1940	George Hall
1886	George Osborne Morgan	1942	Harold Macmillan
1886	Earl of Dunraven	1943	Duke of Devonshire
1887	Earl of Onslow	1945	Arthur Creech-Jones
1888	Baron Henry de Worms	1946	Ivor Bulmer-Thomas
1892	Sydney Buxton	1947	David Rees-Williams
1895	Earl of Selborne	1950	Thomas Cook
1900	Earl of Onslow	1951	Earl of Munster
1903	Duke of Marlborough	1954	Lord Lloyd
1905	Winston Churchill	1957	John Profumo
1908	John Seely	1958	Julian Amery
1911	Lord Lucas	1960	Hugh Fraser
1911	Lord Emmott	1962-4	Nigel Fisher
1914	Lord Islington	1963-4	Richard Hornby
1915	Sir Arthur Steel-Maitland	1964-6	Eirene White
1917	William Hewins	1964-5	Lord Taylor
1919	L.S.Amery	1965-6	Lord Beswick
1921	Edward Wood	1966-7	John Stonehouse

SECRETARY OF STATE FOR THE DOMINIONS

1925	L.S.Amery	1938	Malcolm MacDonald
1929	Lord Passfield	1939	Sir Thomas Inskip (Viscount Caldecote)
1930	J.H.Thomas		
1935	Malcolm MacDonald	1939	Anthony Eden
1938	Lord Stanley	1940	Viscount Caldecote

1940	Viscount Cranborne	1943	Viscount Cranborne
1942	Clement Attlee	1945	Viscount Addison

PARLIAMENTARY UNDER-SECRETARY

1925	Earl of Clarendon	1936	Marquess of Hartingdon (Tenth Duke of Devonshire from 1938)
1927	Lord Lovat		
1929	Earl of Plymouth		
1929	Arthur Ponsonby	1940	Geoffrey Shakespeare
1929	William Lunn	1942	Paul Emrys-Evans
1931	Malcolm MacDonald	1945	John Parker
1935	Lord Stanley	1946	Arthur Bottomley
1935	Douglas Hewitt Hacking		

SECRETARY OF STATE FOR COMMONWEALTH RELATIONS (1947-66)
SECRETARY OF STATE FOR COMMONWEALTH AFFAIRS (1966-8)

1947	Viscount Addison	1952	Viscount Swinton
1947	Philip Noel-Baker	1955	Earl of Home
1950	Patrick Gordon Walker	1960	Duncan Sandys
1951	Lord Ismay	1964	Arthur Bottomley
1952	Marquess of Salisbury (formerly Viscount Cranborne)	1966	Herbert Bowden
		1967	George Thomson

MINISTER FOR COMMONWEALTH RELATIONS (1947)
MINISTER OF STATE FOR COMMONWEALTH RELATIONS (1959-68)

1947	Arthur Henderson	1964-6	Cledwyn Hughes
1959-61	Cuthbert Alport	1966-7	Judith Hart
1962-4	Duke of Devonshire (Eleventh Duke)	1967-8	George Thomas
		1967-8	Lord Shepherd

UNDER-SECRETARY

1947	Arthur Bottomley	1957	Cuthbert Alport
1947	Patrick Gordon Walker	1959	Richard Thompson
1950	Lord Holden	1960-2	Duke of Devonshire (Eleventh Duke)
1950	David Rees-Williams		
1951	Earl of Lucan	1961-2	Bernard Braine
1951	John Foster	1962-4	John Tilney
1954	Douglas Dodds-Parker	1964-6	Lord Taylor
1955	Allan Noble	1965-6	Lord Beswick
1956	Lord John Hope	1967-8	William Whitlock

PRESIDENT OF THE BOARD OF CONTROL

1784	Lord Sydney	1828	Robert Dundas, Viscount Melville
1790	William Wyndham Grenville		
1793	Henry Dundas	1828	Lord Ellenborough
1801	Viscount Lewisham	1830	Charles Grant
1802	Viscount Castlereagh	1834	Lord Ellenborough
1806	Lord Minto	1835	Sir John Cam Hobhouse
1806	Thomas Grenville	1841	Lord Ellenborough
1806	George Tierney	1841	Lord Fitzgerald
1807	Robert Dundas	1843	Earl of Ripon
1809	Earl of Harrowby	1846	Sir John Cam Hobhouse
1809	Robert Dundas	1852	Fox Maule
1812	Earl of Buckinghamshire	1852	J.C.Herries
1816	George Canning	1852	Sir Charles Wood
1821	Charles Bathurst	1855	Robert Vernon Smith
1822	C.W.Williams Wynn	1858	Earl of Ellenborough
		1858	Lord Stanley

Office abolished and replaced by Secretary of State for India in 1858.

SECRETARY TO THE BOARD OF CONTROL

1784	C.W.Boughton Rouse	1839	Lord Seymour and William Clay
1791	Henry Beaufoy		
1793	William Broderick	1841	Charles Buller, vice Seymour
1803	Benjamin Hobhouse		
1804	George Peter Holford	1841	James Emerson Tennant and William Bingham Baring
1806	Thomas Creevey		
1807	George Peter Holford	1845	Viscount Jocelyn and Viscount Mahon
1810	Sir Patrick Murray		
1812	John Bruce	1846	George Stevens Byng and Thomas Wyse
1812	Thomas Peregrine Courtney		
1829	George Bankes	1847	George Cornewall Lewis, vice Byng
1830	John Stuart Wortley		
1830	Lord Sandon	1848	James Wilson, vice Lewis
1831	Thomas Hyde Villiers	1849	John Edmund Elliot, vice Wyse
1832	Thomas Babington Macaulay		
1833	Robert Gordon	1852	Henry James Baillie and C.L.Cumming Bruce
1834	James Alexander Stewart Mackenzie, additionally		
		1852	Robert Lowe and Sir Thomas Redington
1834	Winthrop Mackworth Praed		
1835	Sidney Herbert, additionally	1855	Henry Danby Seymour, vice Lowe
1835	Robert Gordon and Robert Vernon Smith	1857	Sir George Russell Clerk, vice Redington

SECRETARY OF STATE FOR INDIA TO 1937, INDIA AND BURMA 1937-47, BURMA 1947-8

1858	Lord Stanley	1878	Viscount Cranbrook
1859	Sir Charles Wood	1880	Marquess of Hartington
1866	Earl de Grey and Ripon	1882	Earl of Kimberley
1866	Viscount Cranborne	1885	Lord Randolph Churchill
1867	Sir Stafford Northcote	1886	Earl of Kimberley
1868	Duke of Argyll	1886	Viscount Cross
1874	Marquess of Salisbury (formerly Viscount Cranborne)	1892	Earl of Kimberley
		1894	Sir Henry H.Fowler

1895	Lord George Hamilton	1924	Lord Olivier
1903	St John Brodrick	1924	Earl of Birkenhead
1905	Viscount Morley	1928	Viscount Peel
1910	Earl of Crewe	1929	William Wedgwood Benn
1911	Viscount Morley	1931	Sir Samuel Hoare
1911	Earl of Crewe	1935	Marquess of Zetland
1915	Austen Chamberlain	1940	L.S.Amery
1917	Edwin Montagu	1945	Lord Pethick-Lawrence
1922	Viscount Peel	1947	Earl of Listowel

UNDER-SECRETARY OF STATE FOR INDIA

1858	Henry James Baillie	1905	Marquess of Bath
1859	Thomas George Baring	1905	John Ellis
1864	Frederick Temple	1907	Charles Hobhouse
1866	Sir James Fergusson	1908	Thomas Buchanan
1867	Lord Clinton	1909	Master of Elibank
1869	Mountstuart Elphinstone Grant-Duff	1910	Edwin Montagu
		1914	Charles Roberts
1874	Lord George Hamilton	1915	Lord Islington
1878	Edward Stanhope	1919	Lord Sinha
1880	Viscount Enfield	1920	Earl of Lytton
1883	John Kynaston Cross	1922	Earl Winterton
1885	Lord Harris	1924	Robert Richards
1886	Sir Ughtred James Kay-Shuttleworth	1924	Earl Winterton
		1929	Drummond Shiels
1886	Edward Stafford Howard	1929	Earl Russell
1886	Sir John Eldon Gorst	1931	Lord Snell
1891	George Nathaniel Curzon	1931	Marquess of Lothian
1892	G.W.E.Russell	1932	R.A.Butler
1894	Lord Reay	1937	Lord Stanley
1895	Earl of Onslow	1938	Anthony Muirhead
1900	Earl of Hardwicke	1939	Sir Hugh O'Neill
1902	Earl Percy	1940	Duke of Devonshire
1903	Earl of Hardwicke	1943	Earl of Munster

1944   Earl of Listowel   1945   Arthur Henderson

1945   Earl of Scarbrough

SECRETARY FOR TECHNICAL CO-OPERATION (1961-4)

1961   Denis Vosper   1963   Robert Carr

MINISTER OF OVERSEAS DEVELOPMENT (1964-75)
MINISTER FOR OVERSEAS DEVELOPMENT (1975-7)
MINISTER OF STATE (1977-9)

1964   Barbara Castle   1970   Richard Wood

1965   Anthony Greenwood   1974   Judith Hart

1966   Arthur Bottomley   1975   Reginald Prentice

1967   Reginald Prentice   1976   Frank Judd

1969   Judith Hart   1977   Judith Hart

PARLIAMENTARY SECRETARY

1964   Albert Oram   1976   Frank Judd

1969   Benjamin Whitaker   1976   Office vacant

1974   William Price   1977   John Tomlinson

1974   John Grant

WAR OFFICE

SECRETARY OF STATE FOR WAR (from 1794), WAR AND COLONIES (from 1801)

1794	Henry Dundas	1834	Thomas Spring Rice
1801	Lord Hobart	1834	Earl of Aberdeen
1804	Earl Camden	1835	Charles Grant, Lord Glenelg
1805	Viscount Castlereagh		
1806	William Windham	1839	Marquess of Normanby
1807	Viscount Castlereagh	1839	Lord John Russell
1809	Earl of Liverpool	1841	Lord Stanley (formerly Edward Stanley)
1812	Earl Bathurst		
1827	Viscount Goderich	1845	William Ewart Gladstone
1827	William Huskisson	1846	Earl Grey
1828	Sir George Murray	1852	Sir John S.Pakington
1830	Viscount Goderich	1852	Duke of Newcastle
1833	Edward Stanley		

Offices of War and Colonies were divided in 1854.

UNDER-SECRETARY

1794	Evan Nepean	1806	Sir George Shee and Sir James Cockburn
1795	William Huskisson		
1801	John Sullivan	1807	Edward Cooke, vice Shee
1804	Edward Cooke	1807	Charles William Stewart, vice Cockburn

1809	Frederick Robinson, vice Stewart	1833	J.G.Shaw-Lefevre
1809	Cecil Jenkinson, vice Cooke	1834	Sir George Grey
		1835	John Stuart Wortley
		1835	William Ewart Gladstone
1809-16	Henry Edward Bunbury	1835	Sir George Grey
1810	Robert Peel, vice Jenkinson	1839	Henry Labouchere
		1839	Robert Vernon Smith
1812	Henry Goulburn	1841	George William Hope
1821	Robert Wilmot Horton	1846	Lord Lyttelton
1827	Edward Stanley	1846	Benjamin Hawes
1828	Lord Francis Leveson Gower	1851	Frederick Peel
1828	Horace Twiss	1852	Earl of Desart
1830	Viscount Howick	1852	Frederick Peel

SECRETARY OF STATE FOR WAR

1854	Duke of Newcastle	1905	Richard Haldane
1855	Lord Panmure	1912	John Seely
1858	Jonathan Peel	1914	Herbert H.Asquith
1859	Sidney Herbert	1914	Earl Kitchener
1861	Sir George Cornewall Lewis	1916	David Lloyd George
1863	Earl de Grey and Ripon	1916	Earl of Derby
1866	Marquess of Hartington	1918	Viscount Milner
1867	Sir John S.Pakington	1919	Winston Churchill
1868	Edward Cardwell	1921	Sir Laming Worthington-Evans
1874	Gathorne Hardy		
1878	Frederick A.Stanley	1922	Earl of Derby
1880	H.C.E.Childers	1924	Stephen Walsh
1882	Marquess of Hartington	1924	Sir Laming Worthington-Evans
1885	W.H.Smith		
1886	Henry Campbell-Bannerman	1929	Tom Shaw
1887	Edward Stanhope	1931	Marquess of Crewe
1892	Henry Campbell-Bannerman	1931	Viscount Hailsham
1895	Marquess of Lansdowne	1935	Viscount Halifax
1900	St John Brodrick	1935	Alfred Duff Cooper
1903	Hugh Arnold-Forster	1937	Leslie Hore-Belisha

1940	Oliver Stanley	1950	John Strachey
1940	Anthony Eden	1951	Antony Head
1940	David Margesson	1956	John Hare
1942	Sir James Grigg	1958	Christopher Soames
1945	John James Lawson	1960	John Profumo
1946	Frederick Bellenger	1963	Joseph Godber
1947	Emanuel Shinwell	1963	James Ramsden

Office abolished in 1964.

UNDER-SECRETARY

1855	Frederick Peel	1908	Lord Lucas
1857	Sir John William Ramsden	1911	John Seely
1858	Lord Hardinge	1912	Harold Tennant
1859	Earl De Grey and Ripon	1916	Earl of Derby
1863	Marquess of Hartington	1916	Ian Macpherson
1866	Earl of Longford	1919	Viscount Peel
1868	Lord Northbrook	1921	Sir Robert Sanders
1872	Marquess of Lansdowne	1922	Walter Guinness
1874	Earl of Pembroke	1922	Wilfrid Ashley
1875	Earl Cadogan	1924	Clement Attlee
1878	Viscount Bury	1924	Earl of Onslow
1880	Earl of Morley	1928	Duke of Sutherland
1885	Viscount Bury	1929	Earl De La Warr
1886	Lord Sandhurst	1930	Lord Marley
1886	Lord Harris	1931	Earl Stanhope
1890	Earl Brownlow	1934	Lord Strathcona and Mount Royal
1892	Lord Sandhurst		
1895	Lord Monkswell	1939	Earl of Munster
1895	St John Brodrick	1939	Viscount Cobham
1898	George Wyndham	1940-5	Sir Henry Page-Croft
1900	Lord Raglan	1940-2	Sir Edward Grigg
1902	Earl of Hardwicke	1942-3	Arthur Henderson
1903	Earl of Donoughmore	1945	Lord (formerly Sir Henry Page-) Croft
1905	Earl of Portsmouth		

1945   Lord Nathan   1946-7   Lord Pakenham

PARLIAMENTARY SECRETARY (1918-19)

1918   Earl Stanhope

FINANCIAL SECRETARY

1870	J.C.W.Vivian	1915	Henry William Forster
1871	Henry Campbell-Bannerman	1919	Sir Archibald Williamson
1874	Frederick Stanley	1921	George Frederick Stanley
1877	R.J.Loyd-Lindsay	1922	Stanley Jackson
1880	Henry Campbell-Bannerman	1923	Rupert Sackville Gwynne
1882	Sir Arthur Divett Hayter	1924	John James Lawson
1885	Sir Stafford Northcote	1924	Douglas King
1886	Herbert Gladstone	1928	Alfred Duff Cooper
1886	St John Brodrick	1929	Emanuel Shinwell
1892	William Woodall	1930	William Sanders
1895	Joseph Powell Williams	1931	Alfred Duff Cooper
1901	Lord Stanley	1934	Douglas Hewitt Hacking
1903	William Bromley-Davenport	1935	Sir Victor Warrender
1905	Thomas Buchanan	1940	Sir Edward Grigg
1908	Francis Dyke Acland	1940	Richard Law
1910	Charles Edward Mallett	1941	Duncan Sandys
1911	Francis Dyke Acland	1943	Arthur Henderson
1911	Harold Tennant	1945	Maurice Petherick
1912	Harold Baker	1945	Frederick Bellenger
		1946-7	John Freeman

UNDER- AND FINANCIAL SECRETARY

1947	John Freeman	1951	James Hutchison
1947	Michael Stewart	1954	Fitzroy Maclean
1951	Woodrow Wyatt	1957	Julian Amery

1958 Hugh Fraser

1960 James Ramsden

1963 Peter Kirk

SECRETARY AT WAR

1644	Edward Walker	1794	William Windham
1661	Sir William Clarke	1801	Charles Yorke
1666	Matthew Locke	1803	Charles Bragge
1683	William Blathwayte	1804	William Dundas
1692	George Clarke	1806	Richard Fitzpatrick
1704	Henry St John	1807	Sir James Murray Pulteney
1708	Robert Walpole		
1710	George Granville	1809	Lord Granville Leveson Gower
1712	Sir William Wyndham		
1713	Francis Gwyn	1809	Viscount Palmerston
1714	William Pulteney	1828	Sir Henry Hardinge
1717	James Craggs	1830	Lord Francis Leveson Gower
1718	Viscount Castlecomer		
1718	Robert Pringle	1831	Sir Henry Brooke Parnell
1718	George Treby	1832	Sir John Cam Hobhouse
1724	Henry Pelham	1833	Edward Ellice
1730	Sir William Strickland	1834	J.C.Herries
1735	Sir William Yonge	1835	Viscount Howick
1746	Henry Fox	1839	Thomas Babington Macaulay
1755	Viscount Barrington		
1761	Charles Townshend	1841	Sir Henry Hardinge
1762	Welbore Ellis	1844	Sir Thomas Fremantle
1765	Viscount Barrington	1845	Sidney Herbert
1778	Charles Jenkinson	1846	Fox Maule
1782	Thomas Townshend	1852	Robert Vernon Smith
1782	Sir George Yonge	1852	William Beresford
1783	Richard Fitzpatrick	1852	Sidney Herbert
1783	Sir George Yonge		

From 1852 the office was held by the Secretary of State for War, until 1863 when it was abolished.

PAYMASTER GENERAL OF THE FORCES

1660 Sir Stephen Fox	1783 Edmund Burke
1679 Nicholas Johnson and Charles Fox	1784 William Wyndham Grenville
1682 Charles Fox	1784 William Wyndham Grenville and Lord Mulgrave
1689 Earl of Ranelagh	1789 Lord Mulgrave and Marquess of Graham
1703 John Howe and Charles Fox	
1707 James Brydges	1791 Dudley Ryder and Thomas Steele
1713 Thomas Moore and Edward Nicholas	1800 Thomas Steele and George Canning
1714 Robert Walpole	
1715 Earl of Lincoln	1801 Thomas Steele and Lord Glenbervie
1720 Robert Walpole	
1721 Lord Cornwallis	1803 Thomas Steele and John Hiley Addington
1722 Spencer Compton	
1730 Henry Pelham	1804 George Rose and Lord Charles Henry Somerset
1743 Sir Thomas Winnington	
1746 William Pitt	1806 Earl Temple and Lord John Townshend
1755 Earl of Darlington and Viscount Dupplin	
	1807 Charles Long and Lord Charles Henry Somerset
1757 Henry Fox	
1765 Charles Townshend	1813 Charles Long and Frederick Robinson
1766 Lord North and George Cooke	
	1817 Sir Charles Long
1767 George Cooke and Thomas Townshend	1826 William Vesey Fitzgerald
	1828 John Calcraft
1768 Richard Rigby	1830 Lord John Russell
1782 Edmund Burke	1834 Sir Edward Knatchbull
1782 Isaac Barré	1835 Sir Henry Parnell

Office combined with that of Treasurer of the Navy in 1836 to become Paymaster General.

ADMIRALTY

LORD HIGH ADMIRAL
FIRST LORD OF THE ADMIRALTY

Prior to 1660 the holder of the office was Lord High Admiral and
since that date First Lord of the Admiralty unless otherwise shown.

1540	Lord Russell	1638	Earl of Northumberland (First Lord of the Admiralty from 1642)
1542	Earl of Hertford		
1543	Viscount Lisle		
1547	Lord Seymour	1643	Lord Cottington
1549	Earl of Warwick (formerly Viscount Lisle)	1660	Duke of York (Lord High Admiral)
1550	Lord Clinton	1673	Charles II (Lord High Admiral)
1554	Charles, Lord Howard of Effingham		
		1673	Prince Rupert
1558	Lord Clinton	1679	Sir Henry Capell
1585	William, Lord Howard of Effingham, Earl of Nottingham	1681	Daniel Finch, Earl of Nottingham
		1684	Charles II (Lord High Admiral)
1619	Marquess of Buckingham (Duke from 1623)	1685	James II (Lord High Admiral)
1628	Lord Weston, Earl of Portland (First Lord of the Admiralty)	1689	Earl of Torrington
		1690	Earl of Pembroke and Montgomery
1635	Earl of Lindsay	1692	Lord Cornwallis
1636	William Juxon (First Lord of the Admiralty)	1693	Viscount Falkland

1694   Edward Russell, Earl of Orford

1699   Earl of Bridgwater

1701   Earl of Pembroke and Montgomery (Lord High Admiral from 1702)

1702   Prince George of Denmark (Lord High Admiral)

1708   Earl of Pembroke and Montgomery (Lord High Admiral)

1709   Earl of Orford

1710   Sir John Leake

1712   Earl of Strafford

1714   Earl of Orford

1717   Earl of Berkeley

1727   Viscount Torrington

1733   Sir Charles Wager

1742   Earl of Winchilsea and Nottingham

1744   Duke of Bedford

1748   Earl of Sandwich

1751   Lord Anson

1756   Earl Temple

1757   Earl of Winchilsea and Nottingham

1757   Lord Anson

1762   Earl of Halifax

1763   George Grenville

1763   Earl of Sandwich

1763   Earl of Egmont

1766   Sir Charles Saunders

1766   Sir Edward Hawke

1771   Earl of Sandwich

1782   Viscount Keppel

1782   Viscount Howe

1783   Viscount Keppel

1783   Viscount Howe

1788   Earl of Chatham

1794   Earl Spencer

1801   Earl of St Vincent

1804   Viscount Melville (First Viscount)

1805   Lord Barham

1806   Charles Grey

1806   Thomas Grenville

1807   Lord Mulgrave

1810   Charles Yorke

1812   Viscount Melville (Second Viscount)

1827   Duke of Clarence (Lord High Admiral)

1828   Viscount Melville

1830   Sir James Graham

1834   Lord Auckland

1834   Earl de Grey

1835   Lord Auckland

1835   Earl of Minto

1841   Earl of Haddington

1846   Earl of Ellenborough

1846   Earl of (formerly Lord) Auckland

1849   Sir Francis Thornhill Baring

1852   Duke of Northumberland

1853   Sir James Graham

1855   Sir Charles Wood

1858   Sir John S.Pakington

1859   Duke of Somerset

1866   Sir John S.Pakington

1867   H.T.Lowry Corry

1868   H.C.E.Childers

1871   George J.Goschen

1874	George Ward Hunt	1924	Viscount Chelmsford
1877	W.H.Smith	1924	William Bridgeman
1880	Earl of Northbrook	1929	A.V.Alexander
1885	Lord George Hamilton	1931	Sir Austen Chamberlain
1886	Marquess of Ripon	1931	Sir Bolton Eyres-Monsell
1886	Lord George Hamilton	1936	Sir Samuel Hoare
1892	Earl Spencer	1937	Alfred Duff Cooper
1895	George J.Goschen	1938	Earl Stanhope
1900	Earl of Selborne	1939	Winston Churchill
1905	Earl Cawdor	1940	A.V.Alexander
1905	Lord Tweedmouth	1945	Brendan Bracken
1908	Reginald McKenna	1945	A.V.Alexander
1911	Winston Churchill	1946	Viscount Hall
1915	Arthur Balfour	1951	Lord Pakenham
1916	Sir Edward Carson	1951	James P.L.Thomas
1917	Sir Eric Geddes	1956	Viscount Hailsham
1919	Walter Long	1957	Earl of Selkirk
1921	Lord Lee	1959	Lord Carrington
1922	L.S.Amery	1963	Earl Jellicoe

The office was abolished in 1964.

CIVIL LORD OF THE ADMIRALTY

1832	Henry Labouchere	1859	Samuel Whitbread
1834	Lord Ashley	1863	Marquess of Hartington
1835	Lord Dalmeny	1863	James Stansfeld
1841	H.T.Lowry Corry	1864	H.C.E.Childers
1845	Henry Fitzroy	1866	Henry Fenwick
1846	William Francis Cowper	1866	Lord John Hay
1852	Arthur Duncombe	1866	G.J.Shaw-Lefevre
1852	William Francis Cowper	1866	Charles du Cane
1855	Sir Robert Peel	1868	Frederick Stanley
1857	Thomas George Baring	1868	G.O.Trevelyan
1858	Lord Lovaine	1870	Earl of Camperdown
1859	Frederick Lygon	1874	Sir Massey Lopes

1880 Thomas Brassey	1921 Bolton Eyres-Monsell
1882 George Wightwick Rendel	1922 Marquess of Linlithgow
1885 Ellis Ashmead-Bartlett	1924 Frank Hodges
1886 Robert William Duff	1924 Earl Stanhope
1886 Ellis Ashmead-Bartlett	1929 George Hall
1892 Edmund Robertson	1931 Euan Wallace
1895 Austen Chamberlain	1935 Kenneth Lindsay
1900 Ernest Pretyman	1937 J.J.Llewellin
1903 Arthur Lee	1939 Austin Hudson
1905 George Lambert	1942 Richard Pilkington
1915 Duke of Devonshire	1945 Walter Edwards
1916 Earl of Lytton	1951 Simon Wingfield Digby
1916 Ernest Pretyman	1957 Thomas Galbraith
1919 Earl of Lytton	1959 Ian Orr-Ewing
1920 Earl of Onslow	1963 John Hay

SECOND CIVIL LORD (1916-19)

1916   Arthur Pease

SECRETARY TO THE ADMIRALTY
FIRST SECRETARY TO THE ADMIRALTY
PARLIAMENTARY AND FINANCIAL SECRETARY TO THE ADMIRALTY (from 1886)

1660 William Coventry	1698 Josiah Burchett
1667 Matthew Wren	1702 Josiah Burchett and
1672 Sir John Werden	George Clarke
1673 Samuel Pepys	1705 Josiah Burchett
1679 Thomas Hayter	1741 Josiah Burchett and
1680 John Brisbane	Thomas Corbett
1684 Samuel Pepys	1742 Thomas Corbett
1689 Phineas Bowles	1751 John Clevland
1690 James Southerne	1763 Philip Stephens
1694 William Bridgeman	1795 Evan Nepean
1694 William Bridgeman and	1804 William Marsden
Josiah Burchett	

1807	William Wellesley Pole	1895	William Grey Macartney
1809	John Wilson Croker	1900	Hugh Arnold-Foster
1830	George Elliot	1903	Ernest Pretyman
1834	George Robert Dawson	1905	Edmund Robertson
1835	Charles Wood	1908	Thomas Macnamara
1839	Richard More O'Ferrall	1920	Sir James Craig
1841	John Parker	1921	L.S.Amery
1841	Sidney Herbert	1922	Bolton Eyres-Monsell
1845	H.T.Lowry Corry	1923	Archibald Boyd-Carpenter
1846	Henry George Ward	1924	Charles Ammon
1849	John Parker	1924	J.C.C.Davidson
1852	Augustus O'Brien Stafford	1926	Cuthbert Morley Headlam
1853	Ralph Bernal Osborne	1929	Charles Ammon
1858	H.T.Lowry-Corry	1931	Earl Stanhope
1859	Lord Clarence Paget	1931	Lord Stanley
1866	Thomas George Baring	1935	Sir Victor Warrender
1866	Lord Henry Gordon-Lennox	1935	Lord Stanley
1868	William Edward Baxter	1937	Geoffrey Shakespeare
1871	G.J.Shaw-Lefevre	1940	Sir Victor Warrender (Lord Bruntisfield from 1942)
1874	Algernon Egerton		
1880	G.J.Shaw-Lefevre		
1880	G.O.Trevelyan	1945	John Dugdale
1882	Henry Campbell-Bannerman	1950	James Callaghan
1884	Thomas Brassey	1951	Allan Noble
1885	C.T.Ritchie	1955	George Ward
1886	John Tomlinson Hibbert	1957	Christopher Soames
1886	Arthur Bower Forwood	1958	Robert Allan
1892	Sir Ughtred James Kay-Shuttleworth	1959	Ian Orr-Ewing

ADDITIONAL PARLIAMENTARY SECRETARY TO THE ADMIRALTY (1917-19)

1917   Earl of Lytton

FINANCIAL SECRETARY TO THE ADMIRALTY (1942-5)

1942 George Hall   1943 James P.L.Thomas

TREASURER OF THE NAVY

1660	Sir George Carteret	1762	Viscount Barrington
1667	Earl of Anglesey	1765	Viscount Howe
1672	Sir Thomas Osborne	1770	Sir Gilbert Elliot
1673	Sir Edward Seymour	1777	Welbore Ellis
1681	Viscount Falkland	1782	Isaac Barré
1689	Edward Russell	1782	Henry Dundas
1699	Sir Thomas Littleton	1783	Charles Townshend
1710	Robert Walpole	1784	Henry Dundas
1711	Charles Caesar	1800	Dudley Ryder
1714	John Aislabie	1801	Charles Bragge
1718	Richard Hampden	1803	George Tierney
1720	Sir George Byng	1804	George Canning
1724	Pattee Byng	1806	Richard Brinsley Sheridan
1734	Arthur Onslow	1807	George Rose
1742	Thomas Clutterbuck	1818	Frederick Robinson
1742	Sir Charles Wager	1823	William Huskisson
1743	Sir John Rushout	1827	Charles Grant
1744	George Bubb Dodington	1828	William Vesey Fitzgerald
1749	Henry Bilson Legge	1830	Thomas Frankland Lewis
1754	George Grenville	1830	Charles Poulett Thomson
1756	George Bubb Dodington	1834	Viscount Lowther
1756	George Grenville	1835	Sir Henry Parnell

Office combined with that of Paymaster General of the Forces in
1836 to become Paymaster General.

AIR MINISTRY

PRESIDENT OF THE AIR BOARD

1917   Lord Cowdray

PRESIDENT OF THE AIR COUNCIL

1917   Lord Rothermere   1918   Lord Weir

SECRETARY OF STATE FOR AIR

1919	Winston Churchill	1940	Sir Archibald Sinclair
1921	Frederick Guest	1945	Harold Macmillan
1922	Sir Samuel Hoare	1945	Viscount Stansgate
1924	Lord Thomson	1946	Philip Noel-Baker
1924	Sir Samuel Hoare	1947	Arthur Henderson
1929	Lord Thomson	1951	Lord De L'Isle and Dudley
1930	Lord Amulree	1955	Nigel Birch
1931	Marquess of Londonderry	1957	George Ward
1935	Sir Philip Cunliffe-Lister	1960	Julian Amery
1938	Sir Kingsley Wood	1962	Hugh Fraser
1940	Sir Samuel Hoare		

Office abolished in 1964.

PARLIAMENTARY SECRETARY TO THE AIR COUNCIL

1916-19   John Lawrence Baird

UNDER-SECRETARY OF STATE FOR AIR

1919	John Seely	1945-5	Quintin Hogg
1919	George Tryon	1945-5	Earl Beatty
1920	Marquess of Londonderry	1945	John Strachey
1921	Lord Gorell	1946	Geoffrey de Freitas
1922	Duke of Sutherland	1950	Aidan Crawley
1924	William Leach	1951	Nigel Birch
1924	Sir Philip Sassoon	1952	George Ward
1929	Frederick Montague	1955	Christopher Soames
1931	Sir Philip Sassoon	1957	Ian Orr-Ewing
1937	Anthony Muirhead	1959	Airey Neave
1938-44	Harold Balfour	1959	William Taylor
1941-5	Lord Sherwood	1962	Julian Ridsdale
1944-5	Rupert Brabner		

DEFENCE

MINISTER FOR CO-ORDINATION OF DEFENCE

1936 Sir Thomas Inskip   1939 Lord Chatfield

MINISTER OF DEFENCE (1940-64)
SECRETARY OF STATE FOR DEFENCE (from 1964)

1940 Winston Churchill	1964 Denis Healey
1945 Clement Attlee	1970 Lord Carrington
1946 A.V.Alexander	1974 Ian Gilmour
1950 Emanuel Shinwell	1974 Roy Mason
1951 Winston Churchill	1976 Frederick Mulley
1952 Earl Alexander of Tunis	1979 Francis Pym
1954 Harold Macmillan	1981 John Nott
1955 Selwyn Lloyd	
1955 Sir Walter Monckton	
1956 Antony Head	
1957 Duncan Sandys	
1959 Harold Watkinson	
1962 Peter Thorneycroft	

MINISTER OF DEFENCE FOR THE ARMY (1964-7)

1964 James Ramsden   1965 Gerald Reynolds
1964 Frederick Mulley

MINISTER OF DEFENCE FOR THE ROYAL NAVY (1964-7)

1964   Earl Jellicoe   1966   J.P.W.Mallalieu
1964   Christopher Mayhew

MINISTER OF DEFENCE FOR THE ROYAL AIR FORCE (1964-7)

1964   Hugh Fraser   1964   Lord Shackleton

MINISTER OF DEFENCE FOR ADMINISTRATION (1967-70)

1967   Gerald Reynolds   1969   Roy Hattersley

MINISTER OF DEFENCE FOR EQUIPMENT (1967-70)

1967   Roy Mason   1968   John Morris

MINISTER OF STATE FOR DEFENCE PROCUREMENT (1971-2 and from 1981)

1971   Ian Gilmour   1981   Viscount Trenchard

MINISTER OF STATE FOR DEFENCE

1970   Lord Balniel   1981   Viscount Trenchard
1972   Ian Gilmour   1981   Peter Blaker
1974   George Younger
1974   William Rodgers
1976   John Gilbert
1979   Lord Strathcona and
       Mount Royal

UNDER-SECRETARY

1981   Philip Goodhart   1981   Geoffrey Pattie

PARLIAMENTARY SECRETARY (1952-7)

1952	Nigel Birch	1956	Earl of Gosford
1954	Lord Carrington	1957	Lord Mancroft

UNDER-SECRETARY FOR THE ARMY (1964-81)

1964	Peter Kirk	1974	Lord Brayley
1964	Gerald Reynolds	1974	Robert Brown
1965	Merlyn Rees	1979	Bernard Hayhoe
1966	David Ennals	1981	Philip Goodhart
1967	John Boyden	1981	Alfred Wiggin
1969	Ivor Richard		
1970	Ian Gilmour		
1971	Geoffrey Johnson-Smith		
1972	Peter Blaker		
1974	Dudley Smith		

UNDER-SECRETARY FOR THE ROYAL NAVY (1964-81)

1964	John Hay	1976	Albert Duffy
1964	J.P.W.Mallalieu	1979	Keith Speed
1966	Lord Winterbottom		
1967	Maurice Foley		
1968	David Owen		
1970	Peter Kirk		
1972	Anthony Buck		
1974	Frank Judd		

UNDER-SECRETARY FOR THE ROYAL AIR FORCE (1964-81)

1964	Julian Ridsdale	1970	Lord Lambton
1964	Bruce Millan	1973	Anthony Kershaw
1966	Merlyn Rees	1975	Lord Strathcona and Mount Royal
1968	Lord Winterbottom		

1974   Brynmor John
1976   James Wellbeloved
1979   Geoffrey Pattie

MINISTER OF AVIATION SUPPLY (1970-1)

1970   Frederick Corfield

PARLIAMENTARY SECRETARY

1970   David Price

TRADE AND INDUSTRY

PRESIDENT OF THE BOARD OF TRADE

1786	Lord Hawkesbury	1852	Joseph Warner Henley
1804	Duke of Montrose	1852	Edward Cardwell
1806	Lord Auckland (First Baron)	1855	Lord Stanley of Alderley
		1858	Joseph Warner Henley
1807	Earl Bathurst	1859	Earl of Donoughmore
1812	Earl of Clancarty	1859	Thomas Milner Gibson
1818	Frederick Robinson	1866	Sir Stafford Northcote
1823	William Huskisson	1867	Duke of Richmond
1827	Charles Grant	1868	John Bright
1828	William Vesey Fitzgerald	1870	Chichester Samuel Fortescue
1830	J.C.Herries		
1830	Lord Auckland (Second Baron)	1874	Sir Charles Bowyer Adderley
1834	Charles Poulett Thomson	1878	Viscount Sandon
1834	Alexander Baring	1880	Joseph Chamberlain
1835	Charles Poulett Thomson	1885	Duke of Richmond and Gordon
1839	Henry Labouchere		
1841	Earl of Ripon (formerly Frederick Robinson)	1885	Edward Stanhope
		1886	A.J.Mundella
1843	William Ewart Gladstone	1886	Sir Frederick Stanley
1845	Earl of Dalhousie	1888	Sir Michael Hicks-Beach
1846	Earl of Clarendon	1892	A.J.Mundella
1847	Henry Labouchere	1894	James Bryce

1894 James Bryce	1937 Oliver Stanley
1895 C.T.Ritchie	1940 Sir Andrew Duncan
1900 Gerald Balfour	1940 Oliver Lyttelton
1905 Marquess of Salisbury	1941 Sir Andrew Duncan
1905 David Lloyd George	1942 J.J.Llewellin
1908 Winston Churchill	1942 Hugh Dalton
1910 Sydney Buxton	1945 Oliver Lyttelton
1914 John Burns	1945 Sir Stafford Cripps
1914 Walter Runciman	1947 Harold Wilson
1916 Sir Arthur Stanley	1951 Sir Hartley Shawcross
1919 Sir Auckland Geddes	1951 Peter Thorneycroft
1920 Sir Robert Horne	1957 Sir David Eccles
1921 Stanley Baldwin	1959 Reginald Maudling
1922 Sir Philip Lloyd-Greame	1961 Frederick Erroll
1924 Sidney Webb	1963 Edward Heath (also
1924 Sir Philip Lloyd-Greame (changed name to Cunliffe-Lister in 1924)	Secretary of State for Industry, Trade and Regional Development)
	1964 Douglas Jay
1929 William Graham	1967 Anthony Crosland
1931 Sir Philip Cunliffe-Lister	1969 Roy Mason
1931 Walter Runciman	1970 Michael Noble

MINISTER OF STATE

1953 Derick Heathcoat Amory	1964-8 George Darling
1954 Toby Low	1964-5 Edward Redhead
1957 Derek Walker-Smith	1964-7 Roy Mason
1957 John Vaughan-Morgan	1965-70 Lord Brown
1959 Frederick Erroll	1967-8 J.P.W.Mallalieu
1961 Sir Keith Joseph	1968-9 Edmund Dell
1962-3 Alan Green	1968-9 William Rodgers
1962-3 Lord Derwent	1969-70 Goronwy Roberts
1963-4 Lord Drumalbyn (formerly Niall Macpherson)	1970 Frederick Corfield
1963-4 Edward du Cann	

VICE-PRESIDENT OF THE BOARD OF TRADE (to 1868)
PARLIAMENTARY SECRETARY (from 1868)

1786	William Wyndham Grenville	1866	William Monsell
1789	Marquess of Graham	1866	Stephen Cave
1790	Dudley Ryder	1868	G.J.Shaw-Lefevre
1801	Lord Glenbervie	1871	Arthur Wellesley Peel
1804	Nathaniel Bond	1874	G.A.F.Cavendish-Bentinck
1804	George Rose	1875	Edward Stanhope
1806	Earl Temple	1878	John Gilbert Talbot
1807	George Rose	1880	A.Evelyn Ashley
1812	Frederick Robinson	1882	John Holms
1818	Thomas Wallace	1885	Baron Henry de Worms
1823	Charles Grant	1886	C.T.Dyke Acland
1828	Thomas Frankland Lewis	1886	Baron Henry de Worms
1828	Thomas Peregrine Courtenay	1888	Earl of Onslow
1830	Charles Poulett Thomson	1889	Lord Balfour of Burleigh
1834	Viscount Lowther	1892	Thomas Burt
1835	Henry Labouchere	1895	Earl of Dudley
1839	Richard Lalor Sheil	1902	Andrew Bonar Law
1841	Fox Maule	1905	Hudson Kearley
1841	William Ewart Gladstone	1909	Harold Tennant
1843	Earl of Dalhousie	1911	John Robertson
1845	Sir George Clerk	1915	Ernest Pretyman
1846	Thomas Milner Gibson	1916	George Roberts
1848	Earl Granville	1917	George Wardle
1852	Lord Stanley of Alderley	1919	William Bridgeman
1852	Lord Colchester	1920	Sir Philip Lloyd-Greame
1853	Lord Stanley of Alderley	1921	Sir William Mitchell-Thomson
1855	Edward Pleydell Bouverie		
1855	Robert Lowe	1922	Viscount Wolmer
1858	Earl of Donoughmore	1924	A.V.Alexander
1859	Lord Lovaine	1924	Sir Barton Chadwick
1859	James Wilson	1928	Herbert Williams
1859	William Francis Cowper	1929	Walter Smith
1860	William Hutt	1931	Gwilym Lloyd-George
1865	George J.Goschen	1931	Leslie Hore-Belisha

1932	Leslie Burgin	1955	Derek Walker-Smith
1937	Euan Wallace	1956	Frederick Erroll
1938	Ronald Cross	1958	John Rodgers
1939	Gwilym Lloyd-George	1960	Niall Macpherson
1941	Charles Waterhouse	1962	David Price
1945	Ellis Smith	1964	Lord (formerly Hervey) Rhodes
1946	John Belcher		
1949	John Edwards	1967	Lord Walston
1950	Hervey Rhodes	1967	Gwyneth Dunwoody
1951	Henry Strauss	1970	Anthony Grant
1955	Donald Kaberry		

SECRETARY FOR OVERSEAS TRADE (1917-53)

1917	Sir Arthur Steel-Maitland	1931	John Colville
1919	Sir Hamar Greenwood	1935	Euan Wallace
1920	Frederick Kellaway	1937	Robert Hudson
1921	Sir Philip Lloyd-Greame	1940	Geoffrey Shakespeare
1922	Sir William Joynson-Hicks	1940	Harcourt Johnstone
1923	Albert Buckley	1945	Spencer Summers
1924	William Lunn	1945	Hilary Marquand
1924	Arthur Samuel	1947	Harold Wilson
1927	Douglas Hewitt Hacking	1947	Arthur Bottomley
1929	George Gillett	1951	Henry Hopkinson
1931	Sir Edward Hilton Young	1952	Harry Mackeson

SECRETARY FOR MINES DEPARTMENT (1920-42)

1920	William Bridgeman	1930	Emanuel Shinwell
1922	George Lane-Fox	1931	Isaac Foot
1924	Emanuel Shinwell	1932	Ernest Brown
1924	George Lane-Fox	1935	Harry Crookshank
1928	Douglas King	1939	Geoffrey Lloyd
1929	Ben Turner	1940	David Grenfell

SECRETARY FOR PETROLEUM DEPARTMENT (1940-2)

1940   Geoffrey Lloyd

SECRETARY OF STATE FOR TRADE AND INDUSTRY (1970-4)
SECRETARY OF STATE FOR TRADE (from 1974)

1970	John Davies	1981 John Biffen
1972	Peter Walker	
1974	Peter Shore	
1976	Edmund Dell	
1978	John Smith	
1979	John Nott	

MINISTER FOR TRADE (1970-2)
MINISTER FOR TRADE AND CONSUMER AFFAIRS (1972-4)

1970   Michael Noble   1972   Sir Geoffrey Howe

UNDER-SECRETARY

1970   Anthony Grant   1972   Earl of Limerick

MINISTER FOR INDUSTRY (1970-4)

1970   Sir John Eden   1972   Thomas Boardman

UNDER-SECRETARY

1970   Nicholas Ridley   1974   Peter Emery

MINISTER FOR AEROSPACE (1971-2)
MINISTER FOR AEROSPACE AND SHIPPING (1972-4)

1971   Frederick Corfield   1972   Michael Heseltine

UNDER-SECRETARY

1971   David Price   1972   Cranley Onslow

MINISTER FOR INDUSTRIAL DEVELOPMENT (1972-4)

1972   Christopher Chataway

UNDER-SECRETARY

1972   Anthony Grant

MINISTER OF STATE, TRADE

1979   Cecil Parkinson   1981   Peter Rees

UNDER-SECRETARY

1974-6   Eric Deakins
1974-9   Stanley Clinton Davis
1976-9   Michael Meacher
1979-81   Norman Tebbit
1979-   Reginald Eyre
1981-81   Lord Trefgarne
1981-   Iain Sproat

SECRETARY OF STATE FOR PRICES AND CONSUMER PROTECTION (1974-9)

1974   Shirley Williams   1976   Roy Hattersley

MINISTER OF STATE

1974 Alan Williams
1976 John Fraser
1979 Sally Oppenheim

UNDER-SECRETARY (1974-9)

1974 Robert Maclennan

SECRETARY OF STATE FOR INDUSTRY

1974 Anthony Wedgwood Benn
1975 Eric Varley
1979 Sir Keith Joseph
1981 Patrick Jenkin

MINISTER OF STATE

1974-5   Eric Heffer   1981-81 Norman Tebbit
1974-6   Lord Beswick   1981-   Norman Lamont
1975-6   Gregor Mackenzie
1975-9   Gerald Kaufman
1976-9   Alan Williams
1979-81 Adam Butler
1979-81 Viscount Trenchard
1981-   Kenneth Baker

UNDER-SECRETARY

1974-5 Gregor Mackenzie   1974-5 Michael Meacher

1975-5   Gerald Kaufman

1975-6   Lord Melchett

1975-6   Neil Carmichael

1976-9   Leslie Huckfield

1976-8   Robert Cryer

1979-81   David Mitchell

1979-81   Michael Marshall

1981-   John Macgregor

1981-   John Wakeham

MINISTER OF TECHNOLOGY (1964-70)

1964   Frank Cousins

1966   Anthony Wedgwood Benn

1970   Geoffrey Rippon

1970   John Davies

MINISTER OF STATE

1967-8   John Stonehouse

1968-9   J.P.W.Mallalieu

1969-9   Reginald Prentice

1969-70   Lord Delacourt-Smith

1969-70   Eric Varley

1970-70   Sir John Eden

1970   Earl of Bessborough

PARLIAMENTARY SECRETARY

1964-6   Lord Snow

1965-6   Richard Marsh

1966-7   Peter Shore

1966-7   Edmund Dell

1967-9   Jeremy Bray

1967-9   Gerald Fowler

1969-70   Alan Williams

1969-70   Neil Carmichael

1969-70   Ernest Davies

1970-70   David Price

1970-70   Nicholas Ridley

MINISTER OF SUPPLY (1939-59)

1939	Leslie Burgin	1947	George Strauss
1940	Herbert Morrison	1951	Duncan Sandys
1940	Sir Andrew Duncan	1954	Selwyn Lloyd
1941	Lord Beaverbrook	1955	Reginald Maudling
1942	Sir Andrew Duncan	1957	Aubrey Jones
1945	John Wilmot		

PARLIAMENTARY SECRETARY

1939	J.J.Llewellin	1945-7	Arthur Woodburn
1940-2	Harold Macmillan	1947-51	John Freeman
1940-2	Lord Portal	1947-50	John Jones
1942-3	Ralph Assheton	1951	Michael Stewart
1942-5	Charles Peat	1951	Toby Low
1942-4	Duncan Sandys	1954	Sir Edward Boyle
1944-5	John Wilmot	1955	Frederick Erroll
1945-5	James de Rothschild	1956	Ian Harvey
1945	Robert Grimston	1957	William Taylor
1945-7	William Leonard		

MINISTER OF MATERIALS (1951-4)

1951	Richard Stokes	1952	Sir Arthur Salter
1951	Viscount Swinton	1953	Lord Woolton

AGRICULTURE, FISHERIES AND FOOD

PRESIDENT OF THE BOARD OF AGRICULTURE AND FISHERIES

1889	Henry Chaplin	1905	Earl Carrington
1892	Herbert Gardner	1911	Walter Runciman
1895	Walter Long	1914	Lord Lucas
1900	Robert W.Hanbury	1915	Earl of Selborne
1903	Earl of Onslow	1916	Earl of Crawford
1905	Ailwyn Edward Fellowes	1916	Rowland Prothero

MINISTER OF AGRICULTURE AND FISHERIES (AND FOOD since 1954)

1919	Lord Lee	1945	Tom Williams
1921	Sir Arthur Griffith-Boscawen	1951	Sir Thomas Dugdale
		1954	Derick Heathcoat Amory
1922	Sir Robert Sanders	1958	John Hare
1924	Noel Buxton	1960	Christopher Soames
1924	Edward Wood	1964	Frederick Peart
1925	Walter Guinness	1968	Cledwyn Hughes
1929	Noel Buxton	1970	James Prior
1930	Christopher Addison	1972	Joseph Godber
1931	Sir John Gilmour	1974	Frederick Peart
1932	Walter Elliot	1976	John Silkin
1936	W.S.Morrison	1979	Peter Walker
1939	Sir Reginald Dorman-Smith		
1940	Robert Hudson		

MINISTER OF STATE

1972 Anthony Stodart

1974 Norman Buchan

1974 Edward Bishop

1979- Earl Ferrers

1979- Alick Buchanan-Smith

PARLIAMENTARY SECRETARY

1909	Sir Edward Strachey	1940-5	Thomas Williams
1911	Lord Lucas	1941-5	Duke of Norfolk
1914	Sir Harry Verney	1945-5	Donald Scott
1915	Francis Dyke Acland	1945-50	Earl of Huntingdon
1916-19	Sir Richard Winfrey	1945-7	Percy Collick
1917-18	Duke of Marlborough	1947-51	George Brown
1918-18	Viscount Goschen	1950-51	Earl of Listowel
1918-19	Lord Clinton	1951-1	Arthur Champion
1919	Sir Arthur Griffith-Boscawen	1951-4	Lord Carrington
		1951-7	Richard Nugent
1921	Earl of Onslow	1954-7	Earl St Aldwyn
1921	Earl of Ancaster	1955-7	Harmar Nicholls
1924	Walter Smith	1957-60	Joseph Godber
1924	Lord Bledisloe	1958-62	Earl Waldegrave
1928	Earl of Stradbroke	1960-2	William Fletcher-Vane
1929	Christopher Addison	1962-4	Lord St Oswald
1930	Earl De La Warr	1962-4	James Scott-Hopkins
1935	Herwald Ramsbotham	1964-70	John Mackie
1936	Earl of Feversham	1964-70	James Hoy
1939	Lord Denham	1970	Anthony Stodart
1940-1	Lord Moyne	1972	Peter Mills

1972 Peggy Fenner

1974 Earl Ferrers

1974 Roland Moyle

1974 Edward Bishop

1974 Gavin Strang

1979 Alfred Wiggin

1981 Peggy Fenner

MINISTER OF FOOD CONTROL (1916-21)

1916 Viscount Devonport

1917 Lord Rhondda

1918 J.R.Clynes

1919 George H.Roberts

1920 Charles McCurdy

PARLIAMENTARY SECRETARY

1916 Charles Bathurst

1917 J.R.Clynes

1918 Waldorf Astor

1919 Charles McCurdy

1920 Sir William Mitchell-Thomson

MINISTER OF FOOD (1939-54)

1939 W.S.Morrison

1940 Lord Woolton

1943 J.J.Llewellin

1945 Sir Ben Smith

1946 John Strachey

1950 Maurice Webb

1951 Gwilym Lloyd-George

1954 Derick Heathcoat Amory

PARLIAMENTARY SECRETARY

1939 Alan Lennox-Boyd

1940 Robert Boothby

1940 Gwilym Lloyd-George

1942 William Mabane

1945 Florence Horsbrugh

1945 Edith Summerskill

1950 Stanley Evans

1950 Frederick Willey

1951 Charles Hill

EDUCATION AND SCIENCE

VICE PRESIDENT OF THE COMMITTEE OF THE PRIVY COUNCIL ON EDUCATION IN ENGLAND AND WALES

1857	William Francis Cowper	1878	Lord George Hamilton
1858	Charles Bowyer Adderley	1880	A.J.Mundella
1859	Robert Lowe	1885	Edward Stanhope
1864	Henry Austin Bruce	1885	Sir Henry Thurstan Holland
1866	H.T.Lowry-Corry		
1867	Lord Robert Montagu	1887	Sir William Hart Dyke
1868	William Edward Forster	1892	A.H.Dyke Acland
1874	Viscount Sandon	1895	Sir John Eldon Gorst

PRESIDENT OF THE BOARD OF EDUCATION

1900	Duke of Devonshire	1924	Lord Eustace Percy
1902	Marquess of Londonderry	1929	Sir Charles P.Trevelyan
1905	Augustine Birrell	1931	Hastings B.Lees-Smith
1907	Reginald McKenna	1931	Sir Donald Maclean
1908	Walter Runciman	1932	Lord Irwin (formerly Edward Wood)
1911	Joseph Pease		
1915	Arthur Henderson	1935	Oliver Stanley
1916	Marquess of Crewe	1937	Earl Stanhope
1916	H.A.L.Fisher	1938	Earl De La Warr
1922	Edward Wood	1940	Herwald Ramsbotham
1924	Charles P.Trevelyan	1941	R.A.Butler

MINISTER OF EDUCATION

1944 R.A.Butler	1954 Sir David Eccles
1945 Richard Law	1957 Viscount Hailsham
1945 Ellen Wilkinson	1957 Geoffrey Lloyd
1947 George Tomlinson	1959 Sir David Eccles
1951 Florence Horsbrugh	1962 Sir Edward Boyle

SECRETARY OF STATE FOR EDUCATION AND SCIENCE

1964 Quintin Hogg (formerly Viscount Hailsham)	1970 Margaret Thatcher
	1974 Reginald Prentice
1964 Michael Stewart	1975 Frederick Mulley
1965 Anthony Crosland	1976 Shirley Williams
1967 Patrick Gordon Walker	1979 Mark Carlisle
1968 Edward Short	1981 Sir Keith Joseph

PARLIAMENTARY SECRETARY TO THE BOARD/MINISTRY OF EDUCATION

1902 Sir William Reynell Anson	1935 Earl De La Warr
1905 Thomas Lough	1936 Geoffrey Shakespeare
1908 Thomas McKinnon Wood	1937 Kenneth Lindsay
1908 Charles Trevelyan	1940 James Chuter Ede
1914 Christopher Addison	1945 Thelma Cazalet-Keir
1915 Herbert Lewis	1945 Arthur Jenkins
1923 Lord Eustace Percy	1945 David Hardman
1923 Earl of Onslow	1951 Kenneth Pickthorn
1924 Morgan Jones	1954 Denis Vosper
1924 Duchess of Atholl	1957 Sir Edward Boyle
1929 Morgan Jones	1959 Kenneth Thompson
1931 Sir Kingsley Wood	1962 Christopher Chataway
1931 Herwald Ramsbotham	

PARLIAMENTARY UNDER-SECRETARY FOR EDUCATION

1981 William Waldegrave

MINISTER OF STATE, DEPARTMENT OF EDUCATION AND SCIENCE

1964-4	Sir Edward Boyle		1974	Lord Crowther-Hunt
1964-4	Lord Newton		1976	Gerald Fowler
1964-5	Lord Bowden		1976-9	Lord Donaldson
1964-6	Reginald Prentice		1976-9	Gordon Oakes
1965-7	Edward Redhead		1979-	Lady Young
1966-7	Goronwy Roberts		1981-	Paul Channon
1967-9	Shirley Williams			
1967-70	Jennie Lee			
1967-70	Alice Bacon			
1969-70	Gerald Fowler			
1973	Norman St John-Stevas			
1974	Gerald Fowler			

UNDER-SECRETARY

1964-4	Earl of Bessborough		1974-6	Hugh Jenkins
1964-4	Christopher Chataway		1975-6	Joan Lestor
1964-5	James Boyden		1976-9	Margaret Jackson
1964-9	Denis Howell		1979-	Rhodes Boyson
1965-7	Jennie Lee		1979-81	Neil Macfarlane
1969-70	Joan Lestor		1981-	William Shelton
1970-3	Lord Belstead			
1970-2	William Van Straubenzee			
1972-3	Norman St John-Stevas			
1973-4	Lord Sandford			
1973-4	Timothy Raison			
1974-5	Ernest Armstrong			

MINISTER FOR SCIENCE (1959-64)

1959	Viscount Hailsham

PARLIAMENTARY SECRETARY

1961 Denzil Freeth   1963 Earl of Bessborough

HEALTH AND SOCIAL SERVICES

PRESIDENT OF THE POOR LAW BOARD

1847	Charles Buller	1859	Thomas Milner Gibson
1849	Matthew Talbot Baines	1859	Charles Pelham Villiers
1852	Sir John Trollope	1866	Gathorne Hardy
1852	Matthew Talbot Baines	1867	Earl of Devon
1855	Edward Pleydell Bouverie	1868	George J.Goschen
1858	T.H.S.Sotheron-Estcourt	1871	James Stansfeld
1859	Earl of March		

The Poor Law Board became the Local Government Board in 1871.

PRESIDENT OF THE LOCAL GOVERNMENT BOARD

1871	James Stansfeld	1895	Henry Chaplin
1874	George Sclater-Booth	1900	Walter Long
1880	John George Dodson	1905	Gerald Balfour
1882	Sir Charles Dilke	1905	John Burns
1885	Arthur Balfour	1914	Herbert Samuel
1886	Joseph Chamberlain	1915	Walter Long
1886	James Stansfeld	1916	Lord Rhondda
1886	C.T.Ritchie	1918	William Hayes Fisher
1892	Henry H.Fowler	1918	Sir Auckland Geddes
1894	G.J.Shaw-Lefevre	1919	Christopher Addison

The Local Government Board became the Ministry of Health in 1919.

MINISTER OF HEALTH

1919	Christopher Addison	1940	Malcolm MacDonald
1921	Sir Alfred Mond	1941	Ernest Brown
1922	Sir Arthur Griffith-Boscawen	1943	Henry Willink
		1945	Aneurin Bevan
1923	Neville Chamberlain	1951	Hilary Marquand
1923	Sir William Joynson-Hicks	1951	Harry Crookshank
1924	John Wheatley	1952	Iain Macleod
1924	Neville Chamberlain	1955	Robert Turton
1929	Arthur Greenwood	1957	Denis Vosper
1931	Neville Chamberlain	1957	Derek Walker-Smith
1931	Sir Edward Hilton Young	1960	Enoch Powell
1935	Sir Kingsley Wood	1963	Anthony Barber
1938	Walter Elliot	1964	Kenneth Robinson

In 1968 this office was combined with that of the Minister of
Social Security and became Secretary of State for Social Services.

PARLIAMENTARY SECRETARY TO THE POOR LAW BOARD

1847	Viscount Ebrington	1859	Charles Gilpin
1851	Ralph William Grey	1865	Viscount Enfield
1852	Frederick Winn Knight	1866	Ralph Anstruther Earle
1853	Charles Lennox Grenville Berkeley	1867	George Sclater-Booth
		1868	Michael Hicks-Beach
1856	Ralph William Grey	1868	Arthur Wellesley Peel
1858	Frederick Winn Knight		

PARLIAMENTARY SECRETARY TO THE LOCAL GOVERNMENT BOARD (to 1919)
PARLIAMENTARY SECRETARY TO MINISTRY OF HEALTH (from 1919)

1871	John Tomlinson Hibbert	1885	Earl Brownlow
1874	Clare Sewell Read	1886	Jesse Collings
1876	Thomas Salt	1886	William Copeland Borlase
1880	John Tomlinson Hibbert	1886	Walter Long
1883	G.W.E.Russell		Office vacant

1895	Thomas Wallace Russell	1936	Robert Hudson
1900	Sir John Lawson	1937	Robert Bernays
1905	Arthur Jeffreys	1939	Florence Horsbrugh
1905	Walter Runciman	1945	Hamilton Kerr
1907	Thomas Macnamara	1945	Charles Key
1908	C.F.G.Masterman	1947	John Edwards
1909	Herbert Lewis	1949	Arthur Blenkinsop
1915	William Hayes Fisher	1951	Patricia Hornsby-Smith
1917	Stephen Walsh	1957	John Vaughan-Morgan
1919	Viscount Astor	1957	Richard Thompson
1921	Earl of Onslow	1959	Edith Pitt
1923	Lord Eustace Percy	1962-4	Bernard Braine
1924	Arthur Greenwood	1962-4	Lord Newton
1924	Sir Kingsley Wood	1964-4	Marquess of Lothian
1929	Susan Lawrence	1964	Sir Barnett Stross
1931	Ernest Simon	1965	Charles Loughlin
1931	Ernest Brown	1967	Julian Snow
1932	Geoffrey Shakespeare		

PRESIDENT OF THE GENERAL BOARD OF HEALTH

1854	Sir Benjamin Hall	1857	William Francis Cowper
1855	William Francis Cowper	1858	Charles Bowyer Adderley
1857	William Monsell		

The board was abolished in 1858.

MINISTER OF PENSIONS

1916	George Barnes	1924	Frederick Roberts
1917	John Hodge	1924	George Tryon
1919	Sir Laming Worthington-Evans	1929	Frederick Roberts
		1931	George Tryon
1920	Ian Macpherson	1935	Robert Hudson
1922	George Tryon	1936	Herwald Ramsbotham

1939 Sir Walter Womersley	1948 Hilary Marquand
1945 Wilfred Paling	1951 George Isaacs
1947 John Hynd	1951 Derick Heathcoat Amory
1947 George Buchanan	

PARLIAMENTARY SECRETARY

1916 Sir Arthur Griffith-Boscawen	1932 Office vacant
	1940 Ellen Wilkinson
1919 Sir James Craig	1940 Lord (formerly George) Tryon
1920 George Tryon	
1923 Charles Craig	1941 Wilfred Paling
1924 Office vacant	1945 Lord De L'Isle and Dudley
1924 John Muir	1945 Janet Adamson
1924 George Stanley	1946 Arthur Blenkinsop
1929 Office vacant	1949 Charles Simmons
1931 Cuthbert Headlam	1951 John Smyth

MINISTER OF SOCIAL INSURANCE (1944)
MINISTER OF NATIONAL INSURANCE (1944-53)

1944 Sir William Jowitt	1950 Edith Summerskill
1945 Leslie Hore-Belisha	1951 Osbert Peake
1945 James Griffiths	

PARLIAMENTARY SECRETARY

1945 Charles Peat	1950 Bernard Taylor
1945 George Lindgren	1951 Robert Turton
1946 Thomas Steele	

MINISTER OF PENSIONS AND NATIONAL INSURANCE

1953 Osbert Peake	1955 John Boyd-Carpenter

1962   Niall Macpherson   1964   Margaret Herbison

1963   Richard Wood

PARLIAMENTARY SECRETARY

1951-5   John Smyth   1960-1   Bernard Braine

1953-4   Robert Turton   1961-2   Richard Sharples

1954-5   Ernest Marples   1961-4   Margaret Thatcher

1955-9   Edith Pitt   1962-4   Spencer Maydon

1955-8   Richard Wood   1964-6   Harold Davies

1958-60   William Vane   1966-6   Norman Pentland

1959-61   Patricia Hornsby-Smith

MINISTER OF SOCIAL SECURITY

1966   Margaret Herbison   1967   Judith Hart

PARLIAMENTARY SECRETARY

1966-7   Harold Davies   1967-8   Charles Loughlin

1966-8   Norman Pentland

SECRETARY OF STATE FOR SOCIAL SERVICES

1968   Richard Crossman   1981   Norman Fowler

1970   Sir Keith Joseph

1974   Barbara Castle

1976   David Ennals

1979   Patrick Jenkin

MINISTER OF STATE, HEALTH AND SOCIAL SECURITY

1968-9	Stephen Swingler	1979-	Gerard Vaughan
1968-70	David Ennals	1981-	Hugh Rossi
1969-70	Lady Serota		
1970-4	Lord Aberdare		
1974-6	Brian O'Malley		
1974-6	David Owen		
1976-6	Stanley Orme		
1976-9	Roland Moyle		
1979-81	Reginald Prentice		

PARLIAMENTARY UNDER-SECRETARY

1968-9	Norman Pentland	1976-9	Eric Deakins
1968-8	Charles Loughlin	1979-9	Lord Wells-Pestell
1968-9	Julian Snow	1979-81	Sir George Young
1969-70	Brian O'Malley	1979-	Lynda Chalker
1969-70	John Dunwoody	1981-	Lord Elton
1970-4	Paul Dean		
1970-4	Michael Alison		
1974-4	David Owen		
1974-4	Robert Brown		
1974-5	Alec Jones		
1974-9	Alfred Morris		

EMPLOYMENT

MINISTER OF LABOUR

1916	John Hodge	1924	Tom Shaw
1917	George Roberts	1924	Sir Arthur Steel-Maitland
1919	Sir Robert Horne	1929	Margaret Bondfield
1920	Thomas Macnamara	1931	Sir Henry Betterton
1922	Sir Anderson Montague-Barlow	1934	Oliver Stanley
		1935	Ernest Brown

MINISTER OF LABOUR AND NATIONAL SERVICE

1939	Ernest Brown	1951	Alfred Robens
1940	Ernest Bevin	1951	Sir Walter Monckton
1945	R.A.Butler	1955	Iain Macleod
1945	George Isaacs	1959	Edward Heath
1951	Aneurin Bevan		

MINISTER OF LABOUR

1959	Edward Heath	1963	Joseph Godber
1960	John Hare	1964	Raymond Gunter

PARLIAMENTARY SECRETARY TO MINISTRY OF LABOUR

1916	William Bridgeman	1942-5	Malcolm McCorquodale
1919	George Wardle	1945	Ness Edwards
1920	Sir Anderson Montague-Barlow	1950	Frederick Lee
		1951	Sir Peter Bennett
1922	Archibald Boyd-Carpenter	1952	Harold Watkinson
1923	Henry Betterton	1955	Robert Carr
1924	Margaret Bondfield	1958	Richard Wood
1924	Henry Betterton	1959	Peter Thomas
1929	John James Lawson	1961	Alan Green
1931	Milner Gray	1962	William Whitelaw
1931	Robert Hudson	1964-5	Richard Marsh
1935	Anthony Muirhead	1964-6	Ernest Thornton
1937	R.A.Butler	1966-7	Shirley Williams
1938	Alan Lennox-Boyd	1967-8	Ernest Fernyhough
1939-42	Ralph Asheton	1967-8	Roy Hattersley
1941-5	George Tomlinson		

SECRETARY OF STATE FOR EMPLOYMENT AND PRODUCTIVITY

1968   Barbara Castle   1970   Robert Carr

SECRETARY OF STATE FOR EMPLOYMENT

1970   Robert Carr

1972   Maurice Macmillan

1973   William Whitelaw

1974   Michael Foot

1976   Albert Booth

1979   James Prior

MINISTER OF STATE FOR EMPLOYMENT

1969   Edmund Dell   1970   Paul Bryan

1972	Robert Chichester-Clark	1981	Michael Alison
1974	Albert Booth		
1976	Harold Walker		
1979	Earl of Gowrie		

UNDER-SECRETARY OF STATE FOR EMPLOYMENT

1968-9	Ernest Fernyhough	1979-81	James Lester
1968-9	Roy Hattersley	1979-81	Patrick Mayhew
1968-70	Harold Walker	1981-	David Waddington
1970-4	Dudley Smith	1981-	Peter Morrison
1971-2	David Howell		
1974-4	Nicholas Scott		
1974-6	John Fraser		
1974-6	Harold Walker		
1976-9	John Golding		
1976-9	John Grant		

ENVIRONMENT

SECRETARY OF STATE FOR THE ENVIRONMENT

1970   Peter Walker

1972   Geoffrey Rippon

1974   Anthony Crosland

1976   Peter Shore

1979   Michael Heseltine

MINISTER FOR LOCAL GOVERNMENT AND DEVELOPMENT (1970-4)

1970   Graham Page

MINISTER FOR PLANNING AND LOCAL GOVERNMENT (1974-6)

1974   John Silkin

MINISTER FOR TRANSPORT INDUSTRIES (1974)
MINISTER FOR TRANSPORT (1974-6)

1974   John Peyton   1975   John Gilbert

1974   Frederick Mulley

MINISTER FOR HOUSING AND CONSTRUCTION

1970	Julian Amery	1974	Reginald Freeson
1972	Paul Channon		

MINISTER FOR LOCAL AFFAIRS

1979   Thomas King

MINISTER OF STATE

1974   Charles Morris
           (Urban Affairs)

1974-9   Denis Howell
           (Sport and Water
           Resources)

1979-   John Stanley
           (Housing and
           Construction)

UNDER-SECRETARY

1970-4	Eldon Griffiths	1974-5	Neil Carmichael
1970-2	Paul Channon	1974-6	Gordon Oakes
1970-2	Michael Heseltine	1974-9	Lady Birk
1970-3	Lord Sandford	1975-9	Ernest Armstrong
1972-4	Keith Speed	1975-9	Kenneth Marks
1972-4	Reginald Eyre	1976-9	Guy Barnett
1973-4	Lady Young	1979-9	Lady Stedman
1974-4	Hugh Rossi	1979-81	Marcus Fox
1974-5	Gerald Kaufman	1979-81	Geoffrey Finsberg

1979-   Lord Bellwin

1979-81   Hector Monro

1981-   Giles Shaw

1981-   Neil Macfarlane

1981-   Sir George Young

MINISTER OF TOWN AND COUNTRY PLANNING (1942-51)
MINISTER OF LOCAL GOVERNMENT AND PLANNING (1951)
MINISTER OF HOUSING AND LOCAL GOVERNMENT (1951-70)

1942	W.S.Morrison	1961	Charles Hill
1945	Lewis Silkin	1962	Sir Keith Joseph
1950	Hugh Dalton	1964	Richard Crossman
1951	Harold Macmillan	1969	Anthony Greenwood
1954	Duncan Sandys	1970	Robert Mellish
1957	Henry Brooke	1970	Peter Walker

PARLIAMENTARY SECRETARY

1942	Henry Strauss	1961-2	Geoffrey Rippon
1945	Arthur Jenkins	1962-4	Frederick Corfield
1945	Ronald Tree	1962-4	Lord Hastings
1945	Frederick Marshall	1964-7	Robert Mellish
1947	Evelyn King	1964-9	James MacColl
1950	George Lindgren	1966-70	Lord Kennet
1951	Ernest Marples	1967-70	Arthur Skeffington
1954	William Deedes	1969-70	Reginald Freeson
1955	Enoch Powell	1970-70	Paul Channon
1957	Reginald Bevins	1970-70	Eldon Griffiths
1959-61	Sir Keith Joseph	1970-70	Lord Sandford
1959-62	Earl Jellicoe		

MINISTER OF STATE

1957	Lord Brecon (for Welsh Affairs)	1968	Kenneth Robinson (Minister for Planning and Land)
1964	Office vacant		
1967	Frederick Willey	1969	Denis Howell
1967	Neil MacDermot	1970	Graham Page

SECRETARY OF STATE FOR LOCAL GOVERNMENT AND REGIONAL PLANNING (1969-70)

1969   Anthony Crosland

MINISTER OF STATE

1969   Thomas Urwin

MINISTER FOR LAND AND NATURAL RESOURCES (1964-7)

1964   Frederick Willey

PARLIAMENTARY SECRETARY

1964-6 Lord Mitchison   1964-7 Arthur Skeffington

FIRST COMMISSIONER OF WOODS, FORESTS AND LAND REVENUE (1810-51)

1810	Lord Glenbervie	1830	G.J.Welbore Agar Ellis
1814	William Huskisson	1831	Viscount Duncannon
1823	Charles Arbuthnot	1834	Sir John Cam Hobhouse
1827	Earl of Carlisle	1834	Lord Granville Somerset
1827	William Sturges Bourne	1835	Viscount Duncannon
1828	Charles Arbuthnot	1841	Earl of Lincoln
1828	Viscount Lowther	1846	Viscount Canning

1846   Viscount Morpeth (Earl of   1849   Lord Seymour
       Carlisle from 1848)

FIRST COMMISSIONER OF WORKS

1851	Lord Seymour	1894	Herbert Gladstone
1852	Lord John Manners	1895	Aretas Akers-Douglas
1853	Sir William Molesworth	1902	Lord Windsor
1855	Sir Benjamin Hall	1905	Lewis Harcourt
1858	Lord John Manners	1910	Earl Beauchamp
1859	Henry Fitzroy	1914	Lord Emmott
1860	William Francis Cowper	1915	Lewis Harcourt
1866	Lord John Manners	1916	Sir Alfred Mond
1868	Austen Henry Layard	1921	Earl of Crawford
1869	Acton Smee Ayrton	1922	Sir John Lawrence Baird
1873	William Patrick Adam	1924	Frederick Jowett
1874	Lord Henry Gordon-Lennox	1924	Viscount Peel
1876	Gerard James Noel	1928	Marquess of Londonderry
1880	William Patrick Adam	1929	George Lansbury
1881	G.J.Shaw-Lefevre	1931	Marquess of Londonderry
1885	Earl of Rosebery	1931	William Ormsby-Gore
1885	David Robert Plunket	1936	Earl Stanhope
1886	Earl of Morley	1937	Sir Philip Sassoon
1886	Earl of Elgin and Kincardine	1939	Herwald Ramsbotham
		1940	Earl De La Warr
1886	David Robert Plunket	1940	Lord Tryon
1892	G.J.Shaw-Lefevre	1940	Sir John Reith

MINISTER OF WORKS AND BUILDINGS (1940-2)
MINISTER OF WORKS AND PLANNING (1942-3)
MINISTER OF WORKS (1943-62)
MINISTER OF PUBLIC BUILDINGS AND WORKS (1962-70)

1940	Lord (formerly Sir John) Reith	1944	Duncan Sandys
		1945	George Tomlinson
1942	Lord Portal	1947	Charles Key

1950	Richard Stokes	1962	Geoffrey Rippon
1951	George Brown	1964	Charles Pannell
1951	David Eccles	1966	Reginald Prentice
1954	Nigel Birch	1967	Robert Mellish
1955	Patrick Buchan-Hepburn	1969	John Silkin
1957	Hugh Molson	1970	Julian Amery
1959	Lord John Hope		

PARLIAMENTARY SECRETARY

1922-3	Wilfrid William Ashley	1953	Reginald Bevins
1940-5	George Hicks	1957	Harmar Nicholls
1942-2	Henry Strauss	1960	Richard Thompson
1945	Reginald Manningham-Buller	1962	Richard Sharples
		1964	Jenny Lee
1945	Harold Wilson	1965	John Boyden
1947	Evan Durbin	1967	Lord Winterbottom
1948	Lord Morrison	1968	Charles Loughlin
1951	Hugh Molson	1970	Anthony Kershaw

MINISTER OF SHIPPING (1916-21 and 1939-41)

1916	Sir John Maclay	1940	Robert Hudson
1939	Sir John Gilmour	1940	Ronald Cross

PARLIAMENTARY SECRETARY

1916	Sir Leo Chiozza Money	1939	Sir Arthur Salter
1919	Leslie Wilson		

MINISTER OF TRANSPORT (1919-41;   1945-53;   1959-70)
MINISTER OF WAR TRANSPORT (1941-5)
MINISTER OF TRANSPORT AND CIVIL AVIATION (1953-9)
MINISTER FOR TRANSPORT INDUSTRIES (1970-4)
MINISTER FOR TRANSPORT (1974-6)
SECRETARY OF STATE FOR TRANSPORT (1976-9 and from 1981)
MINISTER OF TRANSPORT (1979-81)

1919	Sir Eric Geddes	1954	John Boyd-Carpenter
1921	Viscount Peel	1955	Harold Watkinson
1922	Earl of Crawford	1959	Ernest Marples
1922	Sir John Baird	1964	Thomas Fraser
1924	Henry Gosling	1965	Barbara Castle
1924	Wilfrid Ashley	1968	Richard Marsh
1929	Herbert Morrison	1969	Roy Mason
1931	John Pybus	1970	John Peyton
1933	Oliver Stanley	1974	Frederick Mulley
1934	Leslie Hore-Belisha	1975	John Gilbert
1937	Leslie Burgin	1976	William Rodgers
1939	Euan Wallace	1979	Norman Fowler
1940	Sir John Reith	1981	David Howell
1940	J.T.C.Moore-Brabazon		
1941	Lord Leathers		
1945	Alfred Barnes		
1951	John Maclay		
1952	Alan Lennox-Boyd		

MINISTER OF STATE

1967-8   Stephen Swingler

PARLIAMENTARY SECRETARY

1919	Sir Rhys Rhys-Williams	1924	Office vacant
1919	Arthur Neal	1924	J.T.C.Moore-Brabazon
1922	Wilfrid Ashley	1927	Office vacant
1923	J.T.C.Moore-Brabazon	1929	Earl Russell

1929	Arthur Ponsonby	1957-9	Airey Neave
1931	John Parkinson	1959-63	John Hay
1931	Sir George Gillett	1959-64	Lord Chesham
1931	Earl of Plymouth	1961-4	John Hughes-Hallett
1932	Cuthbert Headlam	1963-4	Thomas Galbraith
1934	Office vacant	1964-6	Lord Lindgren
1935	Austin Hudson	1964-7	Stephen Swingler
1939	Robert Bernays	1966-8	John Morris
1940-1	Frederick Montague	1967-9	Neil Carmichael
1941-2	J.J.Llewellin	1968-70	Robert Brown
1941-2	Sir Arthur Salter	1969-70	Albert Murray
1942-5	Philip Noel-Baker	1970	Michael Heseltine
1945	Peter Thorneycroft	1970-6	Office vacant
1945	George Strauss	1976-9	John Horam
1947	James Callaghan	1979-	Kenneth Clarke
1950	Lord Lucas of Chilworth		
1951-3	J.Gurney Braithwaite		
1952-2	Reginald Maudling		
1952-7	John Profumo		
1953-7	Hugh Molson		
1957-9	Richard Nugent		

MINISTER OF CIVIL AVIATION

1944	Viscount Swinton	1951	Lord Ogmore
1945	Lord Winster	1951	John Maclay
1946	Lord Nathan	1952	Alan Lennox-Boyd
1948	Lord Pakenham		

MINISTER OF TRANSPORT AND CIVIL AVIATION

1953	Alan Lennox-Boyd	1955	Harold Watkinson
1954	John Boyd-Carpenter		

MINISTER OF AVIATION

1959	Duncan Sandys	1964	Roy Jenkins
1960	Peter Thorneycroft	1965	Frederick Mulley
1962	Julian Amery	1967	John Stonehouse

Office became part of Ministry of Technology in 1967.

PARLIAMENTARY SECRETARY FOR CIVIL AVIATION

1945	Robert Perkins	1957-9	Airey Neave
1945	Ivor Bulmer-Thomas	1959-9	John Hay
1946	George Lindgren	1959	Geoffrey Rippon
1950	Frank Beswick	1961	Montague Woodhouse
1951-3	J.Gurney Braithwaite	1962	Basil de Ferranti
1952-2	Reginald Maudling	1962	Neil Marten
1952-5	John Profumo	1964-7	John Stonehouse
1953-5	Hugh Molson	1966-7	Julian Snow
1957-9	Richard Nugent		

ENERGY

MINISTER OF FUEL, LIGHT AND POWER (1942-5)
MINISTER OF FUEL AND POWER (1945-57)
MINISTER OF POWER (1957-69)

1942	Gwilym Lloyd-George	1959	Richard Wood
1945	Emanuel Shinwell	1963	Frederick Erroll
1947	Hugh Gaitskell	1964	Frederick Lee
1950	Philip Noel-Baker	1966	Richard Marsh
1951	Geoffrey Lloyd	1968	Raymond Gunter
1955	Aubrey Jones	1968	Roy Mason
1957	Lord Mills		

PARLIAMENTARY SECRETARY

1942-5	Geoffrey Lloyd	1955	David Renton
1942-5	Tom Smith	1958	Sir Ian Horobin
1945	Sir Austin Hudson	1959	John George
1945	William Foster	1962	John Peyton
1946	Hugh Gaitskell	1964	John Morris
1947	Alfred Robens	1966	Lord Lindgren
1951	Harold Neal	1966	Jeremy Bray
1951	Lancelot Joynson-Hicks	1967	Reginald Freeson

SECRETARY OF STATE FOR THE CO-ORDINATION OF TRANSPORT, FUEL AND POWER

1951-3   Lord Leathers

SECRETARY OF STATE FOR ENERGY

1974   Lord Carrington

1974   Eric Varley

1975   Anthony Wedgwood Benn

1979   David Howell

1981   Nigel Lawson

MINISTER FOR ENERGY

1974   Patrick Jenkin

MINISTER OF STATE

1974   David Howell

1974-6   Lord Balogh

1975-6   John Smith

1976-9   J.Dickson Mabon

1979   Hamish Gray

PARLIAMENTARY UNDER-SECRETARY

1974   Peter Emery

1974-4   Gavin Strang

1974-9   Alex Eadie

1974-5   John Smith

1975-6   Lord Lovell-Davis

1976-6   Gordon Oakes

1979-81 Norman Lamont

1979-   John Moore

1981-   David Mellor

POSTMASTER-GENERAL

POSTMASTER-GENERAL

1655	John Thurloe	1763-5	Robert Hyde
1660	Henry Bishop	1765-6	Lord Grantham
1663	Daniel O'Neale	1766-8	Earl of Hillsborough
1664	Katherine O'Neale, Countess of Chesterfield	1766-81	Lord Le Despencer
		1768-71	Earl of Sandwich
1667	Earl of Arlington	1771-89	Lord Carteret
1685	Earl of Rochester	1782-2	Viscount Barrington
1689	John Wildman	1782-3	Earl of Tankerville
1691-1708	Sir Robert Cotton	1783-4	Lord Foley
1691-1715	Sir Thomas Frankland	1784-6	Earl of Tankerville
1708-15	Sir John Evelyn	1786-6	Earl of Clarendon
1715-20	Lord Cornwallis	1787-94	Lord Walsingham
1715-20	James Craggs	1789-90	Earl of Westmorland
1720-39	Edward Carteret	1790-8	Earl of Chesterfield
1720-5	Galfridus Walpole	1794-9	Earl of Leicester
1725-32	Edward Harrison	1798-1804	Lord Auckland
1733-59	Lord Lovel, Earl of Leicester	1799-1801	Lord Gower
		1801-6	Lord Charles Spencer
1739-44	Sir John Eyles	1804-6	Duke of Montrose
1745-58	Sir Everard Fawkener	1806-7	Earl of Buckinghamshire
1759-62	Earl of Bessborough		
1762-5	Robert Hampden	1806-7	Earl of Carysfort
1762-3	Earl of Egmont	1807-14	Earl of Sandwich

1807-23	Earl of Chichester	1900	Marquess of Londonderry
1814-16	Earl of Clancarty	1902	Austen Chamberlain
1916-23	Marquess of Salisbury	1903	Lord Stanley
1823-6	Earl of Chichester (sole PMG from 1823)	1905	Sydney Buxton
		1910	Herbert Samuel
1826	Lord Frederick Montague	1914	Charles Hobhouse
1827	Duke of Manchester	1915	Herbert Samuel
1830	Duke of Richmond	1916	Joseph Pease
1834	Marquess of Conyngham	1916	Albert Illingworth
1834	Lord Maryborough	1921	Frederick Kellaway
1835	Marquess of Conyngham	1922	Neville Chamberlain
1835	Earl of Lichfield	1923	Sir William Joynson-Hicks
1841	Viscount Lowther, Earl of Lonsdale	1923	Sir Laming Worthington-Evans
1845	Earl of St Germans	1924	Vernon Hartshorn
1846	Marquess of Clanricarde	1924	Sir William Mitchell-Thomson
1852	Earl of Hardwicke		
1853	Viscount Canning	1929	Hastings Lees-Smith
1855	Duke of Argyll	1931	Clement Attlee
1858	Lord Colchester	1931	William Ormsby-Gore
1859	Earl of Elgin	1931	Sir Kingsley Wood
1860	Duke of Argyll	1935	George Tryon
1860	Lord Stanley of Alderley	1940	W.S.Morrison
1866	Duke of Montrose	1942	Harry Crookshank
1868	Marquess of Hartington	1945	Earl of Listowel
1871	William Monsell	1947	Wilfred Paling
1873	Lyon Playfair	1950	Ness Edwards
1874	Lord John Manners	1951	Earl De La Warr
1880	Henry Fawcett	1955	Charles Hill
1884	G.J.Shaw-Lefevre	1957	Ernest Marples
1885	Lord John Manners	1959	Reginald Bevins
1886	Lord Wolverton	1964	Anthony Wedgwood Benn
1886	Henry Cecil Raikes	1966	Edward Short
1891	Sir James Fergusson	1968	Roy Mason
1892	Arnold Morley	1968	John Stonehouse
1895	Duke of Norfolk		

ASSISTANT POSTMASTER-GENERAL

1910	Sir Henry Norman	1942	Robert Grimston
1910	Cecil Norton	1945	William Anstruther-Gray
1915	Herbert Pike Pease	1945	Wilfrid Burke
1924	Viscount Wolmer	1947	Charles Hobson
1929	Samuel Viant	1951	David Gammans
1931	Graham White	1955	Cuthbert Alport
1932	Sir Ernest Bennett	1957	Kenneth Thompson
1935	Sir Walter Womersley	1959	Mervyn Pike
1939	William Mabane	1963	Ray Mawby
1939	Charles Waterhouse	1964	Joseph Slater
1941	Allan Chapman		

MINISTER FOR POSTS AND TELECOMMUNICATIONS

1969	John Stonehouse	1972	Sir John Eden
1970	Christopher Chataway	1974	Anthony Wedgwood Benn

PARLIAMENTARY SECRETARY

1969	Joseph Slater	1969	Norman Pentland

MINISTER WITHOUT PORTFOLIO

Ministers bearing this title are listed from 1830. Frequently in the eighteenth century ministers were included in the cabinet personally rather than by the office, often a sinecure, that they held and these could in some sense be regarded as Ministers Without Portfolio.

1830-4	Earl of Carlisle	1939-40	Lord Hankey
1841-6	Duke of Wellington	1940-2	Arthur Greenwood
1852-8	Marquess of Lansdowne	1942-4	Sir William Jowitt
1853-4	Lord John Russell	1946	A.V.Alexander
1867-8	Spencer Walpole	1947	Arthur Greenwood
1887-8	Sir Michael Hicks-Beach	1954-7	Earl of Munster
1915-16	Marquess of Lansdowne	1957-8	Lord Mancroft
1916-17	Arthur Henderson	1958-61	Earl of Dundee
1916-18	Viscount Milner	1961-2	Lord Mills
1917-18	Sir Edward Carson	1962-4	William Deedes
1917-20	George Barnes	1963-4	Lord Carrington
1917-19	Jan Smuts	1964-6	Eric Fletcher
1918-19	Austen Chamberlain	1964-7	Lord Champion
1919	Sir Eric Geddes	1966-7	Douglas Houghton
1920-1	Sir Laming Worthington-Evans	1967	Patrick Gordon Walker
		1967-8	Lord Shackleton
1921	Christopher Addison	1968-9	George Thomson
1935	Anthony Eden	1969-70	Peter Shore
1935-6	Lord Eustace Percy	1970-4	Lord Drumalbyn
1939	Leslie Burgin	1974	Lord Aberdare

LAW OFFICERS

ATTORNEY-GENERAL

1253-67	Lawrence del Brok	1315-16	William de Herle
	John de Lythegrenes	1315-16	Geoffrey le Scrope
1277-8	William de Boneville	1318-19	Adam de Fyncham
1278-9	William de Giselham	1320-1	Geoffrey le Scrope
1279-80	Gilbert de Thornton	1322-3	Geoffrey de Fyngale
1280-1	Alan de Walkingham	1327	Adam de Fyncham
1281-2	John le Falconer	1327	Alexander de Hadenham
1284-5	William de Seleby	1327	William de Mershton
1286-7	William Inge	1329	Richard de Aldeburgh
1289-90	John de Bosco	1334	Simon de Trewythosa
1289-90	Nicholas de Warwick	1334	William de Hopton or Hepton
1289-90	John de Haydell		
1291-2	Richard de Bretville	1338	John de Lincoln
1291-2	Hugh de Louther	1338	John de Clone or Clove
1292-3	Roger de Hegham	1338	William de Merington
1293-4	John de Mutford	1339	John de Clone or Clove
1300-1	John de Chester	1342	William de Thorpe
1304-5	John de Drokenesford	1343	John de Lincoln
1307-8	John de Chester	1343	John de Clone or Clove
1309-10	Matthew de Scaccario	1349	Simon de Kegworth
1312-13	John de Norton	1353	Henry de Greystoke
1315-16	William de Langley	1356	John Gaunt
1315-16	Gilbert de Toutheby	1360	Richard de Friseby

1362	William de Pleste	1545	Henry Bradshaw
1363	William de Nessefield	1552	Edward Griffin
1366	Thomas de Shardelow	1559	Sir Gilbert Gerrard
1367	John de Ashwell	1581	Sir John Popham
1367	Michael Skilling	1592	Sir Thomas Egerton
1378	Thomas de Shardelow	1594	Sir Edward Coke
1381	William Ellis	1606	Sir Henry Hobart
1381	Laurence Dru	1613	Sir Francis Bacon
1384	William de Horneby	1617	Sir Henry Yelverton
1386	Edmund Brudenell	1621	Sir Thomas Coventry
1398	Thomas Coveley	1625	Sir Robert Heath
1399	William de Lodington	1631	William Noy
1401	Thomas Coveley	1634	Sir John Banks
1401	Thomas Dereham	1641	Sir Edward Herbert
1407	Roger Hunt	1645	Thomas Gardner
1410	Thomas Tickhill	1649	William Steele
1414	William Babington	1649	Edmund Prideaux
1420	William Babthorp	1659	Robert Reynolds
1429	John Vampage	1660	Sir Geoffrey Palmer
1452	William Nottingham	1670	Sir Heneage Finch
1461	John Herbert	1673	Sir Francis North
1461	Henry Hesill	1675	Sir William Jones
1471	William Huse	1679	Sir Creswell Levinz
1478	William Huddersfield	1681	Sir Robert Sawyer
1483	Morgan Kydwelly	1687	Sir Thomas Powys
1485	William Hody	1689	Sir Henry Pollexfen
1486	James Hubbard or Hobart	1689	Sir George Treby
1509	John Ernle	1692	Sir John Somers
1518	John Fitz-James	1693	Sir Edward Ward
1522	John Roper	1695	Sir Thomas Trevor
1524	Ralph Swillington	1701	Sir Edward Northey
1525	Richard Lyster	1707	Sir Simon Harcourt
1529	Christopher Hales	1708	Sir James Montagu
1535	Sir John Baker	1710	Sir Simon Harcourt
1540	William Whorwood	1710	Sir Edward Northey
1541	William Standford	1718	Sir Nicholas Lechmere

1720	Sir Robert Raymond	1832	Sir William Horne
1724	Sir Philip Yorke	1834	Sir John Campbell
1734	Sir John Willes	1834	Sir Frederick Pollock
1737	Sir Dudley Ryder	1835	Sir John Campbell
1754	William Murray	1841	Sir Thomas Wilde
1756	Sir Robert Henley	1841	Sir Frederick Pollock
1757	Sir Charles Pratt	1844	Sir William Webb Follett
1762	Charles Yorke	1845	Sir Frederick Thesiger
1763	Sir Fletcher Norton	1846	Sir Thomas Wilde
1765	Charles Yorke	1846	Sir John Jervis
1766	William de Grey	1850	Sir John Romilly
1771	Edward Thurlow	1851	Sir Alexander Cockburn
1778	Alexander Wedderburn	1852	Sir Frederick Thesiger
1780	James Wallace	1852	Sir Alexander Cockburn
1782	Lloyd Kenyon	1856	Sir Richard Bethell
1783	James Wallace	1858	Sir Fitzroy Kelly
1783	John Lee	1859	Sir Richard Bethell
1783	Lloyd Kenyon	1861	Sir William Atherton
1784	Richard Pepper Arden	1863	Sir Roundell Palmer
1788	Sir Archibald Macdonald	1866	Sir Hugh MacCalmont Cairns
1793	Sir John Scott		
1799	Sir John Mitford	1866	Sir John Rolt
1801	Sir Edward Law	1867	Sir John Burgess Karslake
1802	Spencer Perceval	1868	Sir Robert Porrett Collier
1806	Sir Arthur Pigott		
1807	Sir Vicary Gibbs	1871	Sir John Duke Coleridge
1812	Sir Thomas Plumer	1873	Sir Henry James
1813	Sir William Garrow	1874	Sir John Burgess Karslake
1817	Sir Samuel Shepherd	1874	Sir Richard Baggallay
1819	Sir Robert Gifford	1875	Sir John Holker
1824	Sir John Singleton Copley	1880	Sir Henry James
1826	Sir Charles Wetherell	1885	Sir Richard Everard Webster
1827	James Scarlett		
1828	Sir Charles Wetherell	1886	Charles Arthur Russell
1829	Sir James Scarlett	1886	Sir Richard Everard Webster
1830	Sir Thomas Denman		

1892	Sir Charles Arthur Russell	1936	Sir Donald Somervell
1894	Sir John Rigby	1945	Sir David Maxwell Fyfe
1894	Sir Robert Reid	1945	Sir Hartley Shawcross
1895	Sir Richard Everard Webster	1951	Sir Frank Soskice
		1951	Sir Lionel Heald
1900	Sir Robert Finlay	1954	Sir Reginald Manningham-Buller
1905	Sir John Walton		
1910	Sir Rufus Isaacs	1962	Sir John Hobson
1913	Sir John Simon	1964	Sir Elwyn Jones
1915	Sir Edward Carson	1970	Sir Peter Rawlinson
1916	Sir Frederick Smith	1974	Samuel Silkin
1919	Sir Gordon Hewart	1979	Sir Michael Havers
1922	Sir Ernest Pollock		
1922	Sir Douglas Hogg		
1924	Sir Patrick Hastings		
1924	Sir Douglas Hogg		
1928	Sir Thomas Inskip		
1929	Sir William Jowitt		
1932	Sir Thomas Inskip		

SOLICITOR-GENERAL

1461	Richard Fowler	1552	John Gosnold
1470	Richard Page	1553	William Cordell
1483	Thomas Lynom	1557	Richard Weston
1485	Andrew Dymock	1559	William Roswell
1503	Thomas Lucas	1566	Richard Onslow
1507	John Ernle	1569	Thomas Bromley
1514	John Port	1579	Sir John Popham
1521	Richard Lyster	1581	Sir Thomas Egerton
1525	Christopher Hales	1592	Sir Edward Coke
1531	Baldwin Malet	1595	Thomas Fleming
1533	Richard Rich	1604	Sir John Doderidge
1536	William Whorwood	1607	Sir Francis Bacon
1540	Henry Bradshaw	1613	Henry Yelverton
1545	Edward Griffin	1617	Sir Thomas Coventry

1621	Robert Heath
1625	Sir Richard Sheldon or Shilton
1634	Sir Edward Littleton
1640	Sir Edward Herbert
1641	Oliver St John
1643-5	Sir Thomas Gardner
1645-6	Geoffrey Palmer
1643-8	Oliver St John (Acting Attorney-General from 1644)
1648	Edmund Prideaux
1649	John Cook
1650	Robert Reynolds
1654	William Ellis
1660	Sir Heneage Finch
1670	Sir Edward Turnour
1671	Sir Francis North
1673	Sir William Jones
1674	Sir Francis Winnington
1679	Heneage Finch
1686	Sir Thomas Powys
1687	Sir William Williams
1689	Sir George Treby
1689	John Somers
1692	Sir Thomas Trevor
1695	Sir John Hawkes
1702	Sir Simon Harcourt
1707	Sir James Montagu
1708	Robert Eyre
1710	Sir Robert Raymond
1714	Nicholas Lechmere
1715	John Fortescue Aland
1717	Sir William Thomson
1720	Sir Philip Yorke
1724	Sir Clement Wearg
1726	Charles Talbot
1734	Sir Dudley Ryder
1737	John Strange
1742	William Murray
1754	Sir Richard Lloyd
1756	Charles Yorke
1762	Fletcher Norton
1763	William de Grey
1766	Edward Willes
1768	John Dunning
1770	Edward Thurlow
1771	Alexander Wedderburn
1778	James Wallace
1780	James Mansfield
1782	John Lee
1782	Richard Pepper Arden
1783	John Lee
1783	James Mansfield
1783	Richard Pepper Arden
1784	Archibald Macdonald
1788	John Scott
1793	John Mitford
1799	William Grant
1801	Spencer Perceval
1802	Sir Thomas Manners Sutton
1805	Sir Vicary Gibbs
1806	Sir Samuel Romilly
1807	Sir Thomas Plumer
1812	Sir William Garrow
1813	Sir Robert Dallas
1813	Sir Samuel Shepherd
1817	Sir Robert Gifford
1819	John Singleton Copley
1824	Sir Charles Wetherell
1826	Sir Nicholas Conyngham Tindal

1829	Sir Edward Burtenshaw Sugden	1874	Sir Richard Baggallay
		1874	Sir John Holker
1830	Sir William Horne	1875	Sir Hardinge Stanley Giffard
1832	Sir John Campbell		
1834	Sir Charles Christopher Pepys	1880	Sir Farrer Herschell
		1885	Sir John Eldon Gorst
1834	Robert Monsey Rolfe	1886	Sir Horace Davey
1834	Sir William Webb Follett	1886	Sir Edward Clarke
1835	Sir Robert Monsey Rolfe	1892	Sir John Rigby
1839	Sir Thomas Wilde	1894	Sir Robert Reid
1841	Sir William Webb Follett	1894	Sir Frank Lockwood
1844	Sir Frederick Thesiger	1895	Sir Robert Finlay
1845	Sir Fitzroy Kelly	1900	Sir Edward Carson
1846	John Jervis	1905	Sir William Robson
1846	Sir David Dundas	1908	Sir Samuel Evans
1848	Sir John Romilly	1910	Sir Rufus Isaacs
1850	Sir Alexander Cockburn	1910	Sir John Simon
1851	Sir William Page Wood	1913	Sir Stanley Buckmaster
1852	Sir Fitzroy Kelly	1915	Sir Frederick Smith
1852	Sir Richard Bethell	1916	Sir George Cave
1856	James Stuart Wortley	1916	Sir Gordon Hewart
1857	Sir Henry Singer Keating	1919	Sir Ernest Pollock
1858	Sir Hugh MacCalmont Cairns	1922	Sir Leslie Scott
1859	Sir Henry Singer Keating	1922	Sir Thomas Inskip
1859	Sir William Atherton	1924	Sir Henry Slesser
1861	Sir Roundell Palmer	1924	Sir Thomas Inskip
1863	Sir Robert Porrett Collier	1928	Sir Frank Merriman
1866	Sir William Bovill	1929	Sir James Melville
1866	Sir John Burgess Karslake	1930	Sir Stafford Cripps
1867	Sir Charles Jasper Selwyn	1931	Sir Thomas Inskip
1868	Sir William Baliol Brett	1932	Sir Frank Merriman
1868	Sir Richard Baggallay	1934	Sir Donald Somervell
1868	Sir John Duke Coleridge	1936	Sir Terence O'Connor
1871	Sir George Jessel	1940	Sir William Jowitt
1873	Sir Henry James	1942	Sir David Maxwell Fyfe
1873	Sir William Vernon Harcourt	1945	Sir Walter Monckton

1945 Sir Frank Soskice	1970 Sir Geoffrey Howe
1951 Sir Lynn Ungoed-Thomas	1972 Sir Michael Havers
1951 Sir Reginald Manningham-Buller	1974 Peter Archer
1954 Sir Harry Hylton-Foster	1979 Sir Ian Percival
1959 Sir Jocelyn Simon	
1962 Sir John Hobson	
1962 Sir Peter Rawlinson	
1964 Sir Dingle Foot	
1967 Sir Arthur Irvine	

PARLIAMENTARY SECRETARY TO THE LAW OFFICERS (1974-9)

1974   Arthur Davidson

WARTIME OFFICES

These offices are those instituted during the two world wars and which were wound up during or shortly after the end of the war. Other ministries which originated in wartime but continued, at least for some time, will be found in the relevant sections.

MINISTER OF BLOCKADE (1916-19)

1916	Lord Robert Cecil	1918	Sir Laming Worthington-Evans

PARLIAMENTARY SECRETARY

1916   Frederick Leverton Harris

MINISTER OF INFORMATION (1918-19 and 1939-46)

1918	Lord Beaverbrook	1940	Alfred Duff Cooper
1918	Lord Downham	1941	Brendan Bracken
1939	Lord Macmillan	1945	Geoffrey Lloyd
1940	Sir John Reith	1945	Edward Williams

PARLIAMENTARY SECRETARY

1939	Sir Edward Grigg	1941	Ernest Thurtle
1940	Harold Nicolson		

MINISTER OF NATIONAL SERVICE (1916–19)

1916 Neville Chamberlain	1917 Sir Auckland Geddes

PARLIAMENTARY SECRETARY

1917–17 Stephen Walsh	1918–19 Viscount Peel
1917–19 Cecil Beck	

MINISTER OF MUNITIONS (1915–21)

1915 David Lloyd George	1917 Winston Churchill
1916 Edwin Montagu	1919 Lord Inverforth
1916 Christopher Addison	

PARLIAMENTARY SECRETARY

1915–16 Christopher Addison	1916–21 Frederick Kellaway
1915–16 Arthur Lee	1918–19 John Seely
1916–18 Sir Laming Worthington-Evans	1919–19 John Baird

PARLIAMENTARY AND FINANCIAL SECRETARY

1918 Sir Laming Worthington-Evans	1919–21 James Hope

MINISTER OF RECONSTRUCTION (1917–19 and 1943–5)

1917 Christopher Addison	1943 Lord Woolton
1919 Sir Auckland Geddes	

MINISTER OF ECONOMIC WARFARE (1939-45)

1939   Ronald Cross   1942   Viscount Wolmer
1940   Hugh Dalton

PARLIAMENTARY SECRETARY

1940   Dingle Foot

MINISTER OF AIRCRAFT PRODUCTION (1940-5)

1940   Lord Beaverbrook   1942   Sir Stafford Cripps
1941   J.T.C.Moore-Brabazon   1945   Ernest Brown
1942   J.J.Llewellin

PARLIAMENTARY SECRETARY

1940   J.J.Llewellin   1942   Ben Smith
1941   Frederick Montague   1943   Alan Lennox-Boyd

MINISTER OF STATE (1941-2, became MINISTER OF PRODUCTION)

1941   Lord Beaverbrook   1941   Oliver Lyttelton

MINISTER OF PRODUCTION (1942-5)

1942   Lord Beaverbrook   1942   Oliver Lyttelton

PARLIAMENTARY SECRETARY

1942   George Garro-Jones   1945   John Maclay

MINISTER RESIDENT IN THE MIDDLE EAST (1942-4)

1942 Oliver Lyttelton	1942 R.G.Casey

MINISTER OF STATE IN THE MIDDLE EAST (1944-5)

1944 Lord Moyne	1944 Sir Edward Grigg

DEPUTY MINISTER OF STATE IN THE MIDDLE EAST (1942-4)

1942 Lord Moyne

MINISTER RESIDENT IN SINGAPORE (1941)

1941 Alfred Duff Cooper

MINISTER RESIDENT AT ALLIED HEADQUARTERS IN NORTH WEST AFRICA (1942-5)

1942 Harold Macmillan

MINISTER RESIDENT IN WEST AFRICA (1942-5)

1942 Viscount Swinton	1944 Harold Balfour

MINISTER RESIDENT IN WASHINGTON FOR SUPPLY (1942-5)

1942 J.J.Llewellin	1943 Ben Smith

SCOTLAND

SECRETARY OF STATE FOR SCOTLAND (1709-46 and from 1926)
SECRETARY FOR SCOTLAND (1885-1926)

1709	Duke of Queensberry and Dover	1916	Harold Tennant
		1916	Robert Munro
1713	Earl of Mar	1922	Viscount Novar
1714	Duke of Montrose	1924	William Adamson
1716	Duke of Roxburghe	1924	Sir John Gilmour
1725	Office vacant	1929	William Adamson
1742	Marquess of Tweeddale	1931	Sir Archibald Sinclair
		1932	Sir Godfrey Collins
		1936	Walter Elliot
1885	Duke of Richmond and Gordon	1938	John Colville
		1940	Ernest Brown
1886	G.O.Trevelyan	1941	Thomas Johnston
1886	Earl of Dalhousie	1945	Earl of Rosebery
1886	Arthur Balfour	1945	Joseph Westwood
1887	Marquess of Lothian	1947	Arthur Woodburn
1892	Sir G.O.Trevelyan	1950	Hector McNeil
1895	Lord Balfour of Burleigh	1951	James Stuart
1903	Andrew Graham Murray	1957	John Maclay
1905	Marquess of Linlithgow	1962	Michael Noble
1905	John Sinclair, Lord Pentland	1964	William Ross
		1970	Gordon Campbell
1912	Thomas McKinnon Wood	1974	William Ross

1976   Bruce Millan
1979   George Younger

MINISTER OF STATE

1951 Earl of Home	1974-5 Lord Hughes
1955 Thomas Galbraith, Lord Strathclyde	1975-8 Lord Kirkhill
	1976-9 Gregor Mackenzie
1958 Lord Forbes	1979 Earl of Mansfield
1959 Jack Nixon Browne	
1964-7 George Willis	
1967-70 J.Dickson Mabon	
1969-70 Lord Hughes	
1970 Lady Tweedsmuir	
1972 Lord Polwarth	
1974-6 Bruce Millan	

PARLIAMENTARY SECRETARY TO THE MINISTRY OF HEALTH FOR SCOTLAND (1919-26)

1919 John Pratt	1924 James Stewart
1922 James Kidd	1924 Walter Elliot
1923 Walter Elliot	

UNDER-SECRETARY TO THE SCOTTISH OFFICE

1926 Walter Elliot	1940-5 Joseph Westwood
1929 Thomas Johnston	1941-2 Henry Wedderburn
1931 Joseph Westwood	1942-5 Allan Chapman
1931 Noel Skelton	1945-5 Thomas Galbraith
1935 John Colville	1945-7 George Buchanan
1936 Henry Wedderburn	1945-51 Thomas Fraser
1939 John McEwen	1947-50 John Robertson

1950-1	Margaret Herbison	1967-70	Norman Buchan
1951-5	Thomas Galbraith	1970-4	Alick Buchanan-Smith
1951-5	William Snadden	1970-1	Edward Taylor
1952-7	James Henderson Stewart	1970-4	George Younger
1955-60	Niall Macpherson	1971-4	Hector Monro
1955-9	Jack Nixon Browne	1974-4	Edward Taylor
1957-9	Lord John Hope	1974-4	Robert Hughes
1959-62	Thomas Galbraith (son of Thomas Galbraith, above)	1974-9	Hugh Brown
		1974-9	Harry Ewing
		1975-9	Frank McElhone
1959-63	Gilmour Leburn	1979-	Alex Fletcher
1960-3	Richard Brooman-White	1979-81	Russell Fairgrieve
1962-4	Lady Tweedsmuir	1979-	Malcolm Rifkind
1963-4	Anthony Stoddart	1981-	Allan Stewart
1963-4	Gordon Campbell		
1964-9	Lord Hughes		
1964-6	Judith Hart		
1964-7	J.Dickson Mabon		
1966-70	Bruce Millan		

LORD ADVOCATE

1483-8	Sir John Ross of Montgrenan	1555-73	John Spens of Condie
1490-4	Sir John Ross of Montgrenan	1559-82	Robert Crichton of Eliok and Cluny
1494-1513	James Henderson of Fordell	1573-81	David Borthwick
1503-7	Richard Lawson of Hariggs	1582-96	David Macgill of Cranstonriddel
1507-24	James Wishart of Pittarrow	1594-7	William Hart of Livielands
1524-38	Sir Adam Otterburn	1596-1612	Sir Thomas Hamilton
		1612-28	Sir William Oliphant
1533-59	Henry Lauder of St Germains	1626-46	Sir Thomas Hope
		1646	Sir Archibald Johnston of Warristoun

1649	Sir Thomas Nicolson
1652	Office vacant
1658	Sir George Lockhart of Lee
1661	Sir John Fletcher
1664	Sir John Nisbet of Dirleton
1677	Sir George Mackenzie of Rosehaugh
1681	Sir John Dalrymple
1688	Sir George Mackenzie of Rosehaugh
1689	Sir John Dalrymple
1692	Sir James Stewart
1709	Sir David Dalrymple of Hailes
1711	Sir James Stewart of Goodtrees
1714	Thomas Kennedy of Dunure
1714	Sir David Dalrymple
1720	Robert Dundas of Arniston
1725	Duncan Forbes of Culloden
1737	Charles Erskine of Tinwald
1742	Robert Craigie of Glendoich
1746	William Grant of Prestongrange
1754	Robert Dundas of Arniston (Junior)
1760	Thomas Miller of Glenlee
1766	James Montgomery
1775	Henry Dundas
1783	Henry Erskine
1784	Ilay Campbell of Succoth
1789	Robert Dundas of Arniston (son of the Dundas of 1754)
1801	Charles Hope of Granton
1804	Sir James Montgomery (Junior)
1806	Henry Erskine
1807	Archibald Campbell-Colquhoun
1816	Alexander Maconochie
1819	Sir William Rae
1830	Francis Jeffrey
1834	John Archibald Murray
1834	Sir William Rae
1835	John Archibald Murray
1839	Andrew Rutherfurd
1841	Sir William Rae
1842	Duncan McNeill
1846	Andrew Rutherfurd
1851	James Moncreiff
1852	Adam Anderson
1852	John Inglis
1852	James Moncreiff
1858	John Inglis
1858	Charles Baillie
1859	David Mure
1859	James Moncreiff
1866	George Patton
1867	Edward Strathearn Gordon
1868	James Moncreiff
1869	George Young
1874	Edward Strathearn Gordon
1876	William Watson
1880	John McLaren
1881	John Blair Balfour
1885	John H.A.Macdonald
1886	John Blair Balfour
1886	John H.A.Macdonald
1888	James P.B.Robertson

1891	Sir Charles John Pearson	1941	James Reid
1892	John Blair Balfour	1945	George Thomson
1895	Sir Charles John Pearson	1947	John Wheatley
1896	Andrew Graham Murray	1951	James L.McD.Clyde
1903	Charles Scott Dickson	1954	William Milligan
1905	Thomas Shaw	1960	William Grant
1909	Alexander Ure	1962	Ian Shearer
1913	Robert Munro	1964	Gordon Stott
1916	James Avon Clyde	1967	Henry Wilson
1920	Thomas Morison	1970	Norman Wylie
1922	Charles Murray	1974	Ronald King Murray
1922	William Watson	1979	Lord Mackay of Clashfern
1924	Hugh Macmillan		
1924	William Watson		
1929	Alexander MacRobert		
1929	Craigie Aitchison		
1933	Wilfrid Normand		
1935	Douglas Jamieson		
1935	Thomas Cooper		

SOLICITOR GENERAL FOR SCOTLAND

1587	William Macartney	1689	William Lockhart of Carstairs
1591	William Hart		
1594	James Hamilton	1693	Sir James Ogilvy
1617	James Durham	1699	Sir Patrick Hume of Lumsden
1622-47	James Oliphant		
1626-34	William Haig of Bemerside	1701	Sir David Dalrymple of Hailes and William Carmichael of Skirling
1647-62	Robert Dalgleish		
1662-84	William Purves	1709	Sir James Steuart and Thomas Kennedy
1678-84	John Purves		
1684	George Bannerman and Robert Colt	1714	John Carnegy of Boyseck
		1714	Sir James Steuart
1687	James Graham	1717	Robert Dundas

1720	Walter Stewart
1721	John Sinclair and Charles Binning of Pilmuir
1725	Charles Erskine of Tinwald
1737	William Grant of Prestongrange
1742	Robert Dundas of Arniston (Junior)
1746	Patrick Haldane and Alexander Hume
1755	Andrew Pringle of Alemore
1759	Thomas Miller of Barskimming and Glenlee
1760	James Montgomery and Francis Garden
1764	James Montgomery
1766	Henry Dundas
1775	Alexander Murray of Henderland
1783	Ilay Campbell of Succoth
1783	Alexander Wight
1784	Robert Dundas of Arniston (son of the Dundas of 1742)
1789	Robert Blair of Avonton
1806	John Clerk of Eldin
1807	David Boyle of Shewalton
1811	David Monypenny of Pitmilly
1813	Alexander Maconochie
1816	James Wedderburn
1822	John Hope
1830	Henry Cockburn
1834	Andrew Skene
1834	Duncan McNeill
1835	John Cuninghame
1837	Andrew Rutherfurd
1839	James Ivory
1840	Thomas Maitland of Dundrennan
1841	Duncan McNeill
1842	Adam Anderson
1846	Thomas Maitland of Dundrennan
1850	James Moncreiff
1851	John Cowan
1852	George Deas
1852	Charles Neaves
1853	Robert Handyside
1853	James Craufurd
1854	Thomas Mackenzie
1855	Edward Francis Maitland
1858	Charles Baillie
1858	David Mure
1859	George Patton
1859	Edward Francis Maitland
1862	George Young
1866	Edward Strathearn Gordon
1867	John Millar
1868	George Young
1869	Andrew Rutherfurd Clark
1874	John Millar
1874	William Watson
1876	John H.A.Macdonald
1880	John Blair Balfour
1881	Alexander Asher
1885	James P.B.Robertson
1886	Alexander Asher
1886	James P.B.Robertson
1888	Moir T.Stormonth Darling
1890	Sir Charles John Pearson
1891	Andrew Graham Murray

1892	Alexander Asher	1936	James S.C.Reid
1894	Thomas Shaw	1941	Sir David King Murray
1895	Andrew Graham Murray	1945	Daniel P.Blades
1896	Charles Scott Dickson	1947	John Wheatley
1903	David Dundas	1947	Douglas Johnston
1905	Edward T.Salvesen	1951	William Milligan
1905	James Avon Clyde	1955	William Grant
1905	Alexander Ure	1960	David Colville Anderson
1909	Arthur Dewar	1964	Norman Wylie
1910	William Hunter	1964	James Leechman
1911	Andrew M.Anderson	1965	Henry Stephen Wilson
1913	Thomas Morison	1967	Ewart G.F.Stewart
1920	Charles D.Murray	1970	David Brand
1922	Andrew Briggs Constable	1972	Ian Stewart
1922	William Watson	1974	John McCluskey
1922	David Pinkerton Fleming	1979	Nicholas Fairbairn
1923	Frederick C.Thomson		
1924	John C.Fenton		
1924	David Pinkerton Fleming		
1926	Alexander MacRobert		
1929	Wilfrid Normand		
1929	John C.Watson		
1931	Wilfrid Normand		
1933	Douglas Jamieson		
1935	Thomas Cooper		
1935	Albert Russell		

WALES

MINISTER FOR WELSH AFFAIRS

From 1951 to 1957 this post was held by the Home Secretary, and from 1957 to 1964 by the Minister of Housing and Local Government.

1951	Sir David Maxwell Fyfe	1961	Charles Hill
1954	Gwilym Lloyd-George	1962	Sir Keith Joseph
1957	Henry Brooke		

SECRETARY OF STATE FOR WALES

1964	James Griffiths	1970	Peter Thomas
1966	Cledwyn Hughes	1974	John Morris
1968	George Thomas	1979	Nicholas Edwards

MINISTER OF STATE FOR WELSH AFFAIRS (1957-74)

1957	Lord Brecon	1967	Eirene White
1964	Goronwy Roberts	1970	David Gibson-Watt
1966	George Thomas		

PARLIAMENTARY UNDER-SECRETARY FOR WALES (1964-70, 1974 to date)

1964	Harold Finch	1966	Ifor Davies

1969-70	Edward Rowlands
1974-5	Edward Rowlands
1974-9	Barry Jones
1975-9	Alec Jones
1979-	Michael Roberts
1979-	Wyn Roberts

IRELAND

LORD LIEUTENANT OF IRELAND (from 1801)

1801	Earl of Hardwicke	1858	Earl of Eglinton
1806	Duke of Bedford	1859	Earl of Carlisle
1807	Duke of Richmond	1864	Lord Wodehouse
1813	Earl Whitworth	1866	Marquess of Abercorn
1817	Earl Talbot	1868	Earl Spencer
1821	Marquess Wellesley	1874	Duke (formerly Marquess) of Abercorn
1828	Marquess of Anglesey		
1829	Duke of Northumberland	1876	Duke of Marlborough
1830	Marquess of Anglesey	1880	Earl Cowper
1833	Marquess Wellesley	1882	Earl Spencer
1834	Earl of Haddington	1885	Earl of Carnarvon
1835	Earl of Mulgrave	1886	Earl of Aberdeen
1839	Viscount Ebrington	1886	Marquess of Londonderry
1841	Earl De Grey	1889	Marquess of Zetland
1844	Lord Heytesbury	1892	Lord Houghton
1846	Earl of Bessborough	1895	Earl Cadogan
1847	Earl of Clarendon	1902	Earl of Dudley
1852	Earl of Eglinton	1905	Earl of Aberdeen
1853	Earl of St Germans	1915	Lord Wimborne
1855	Earl of Carlisle	1918	Viscount French
		1921	Lord Fitzalan of Derwent

CHIEF SECRETARY FOR IRELAND (since 1801, until 1922)

1801	Charles Abbot	1859	Edward Cardwell
1802	William Wickham	1861	Sir Robert Peel
1804	Sir Evan Nepean	1865	Chichester Samuel Fortescue
1805	Nicholas Vansittart		
1805	Charles Long	1866	Lord Naas
1806	William Elliot	1868	John Wilson Patten
1807	Sir Arthur Wellesley	1868	Chichester Samuel Fortescue
1809	Robert Dundas		
1809	William Wellesley-Pole	1871	Marquess of Hartington
1812	Robert Peel	1874	Sir Michael Hicks-Beach
1818	Charles Grant	1878	James Lowther
1821	Henry Goulburn	1880	William Edward Forster
1827	William Lamb	1882	Lord Frederick Cavendish
1828	Lord Francis Leveson Gower	1882	G.O.Trevelyan
1830	Sir Henry Hardinge	1884	Henry Campbell-Bannerman
1830	Edward Stanley	1885	Sir William Hart Dyke
1833	Sir John Cam Hobhouse	1886	W.H.Smith
1833	Edward Littleton	1886	John Morley
1834	Sir Henry Hardinge	1886	Sir Michael Hicks-Beach
1835	Viscount Morpeth	1887	Arthur Balfour
1841	Lord Eliot	1891	William Lawies Jackson
1845	Sir Thomas Fremantle	1892	John Morley
1846	Earl of Lincoln	1895	Gerald Balfour
1846	Henry Labouchere	1900	George Wyndham
1847	Sir William Meredyth Somerville	1905	Walter Long
		1905	James Bryce
1852	Lord Naas	1907	Augustine Birrell
1852	Sir John Young	1916	Sir Henry Duke
1855	Edward Horsman	1918	Edward Shortt
1857	Henry Arthur Herbert	1919	Ian Macpherson
1858	Lord Naas	1920	Sir Hamar Greenwood

VICE-PRESIDENT OF THE DEPARTMENT OF AGRICULTURE FOR IRELAND (1899-1922)

1899	Sir Horace Plunkett	1919	Hugh Barrie
1907	Thomas Russell		

LORD CHANCELLOR OF IRELAND (from 1801, until 1922)

1789	Earl of Clare	1867	Abraham Brewster
1802	Lord Redesdale	1868	Lord O'Hagan
1806	George Ponsonby	1874	In commission
1807	Lord Manners	1875	John Thomas Ball
1827	Sir Anthony Hart	1880	Lord O'Hagan
1830	Lord Plunket	1881	Hugh Law
1835	Sir Edward Burtenshaw Sugden	1883	Sir Edward Sullivan
		1885	John Naish
1835	Lord Plunket	1885	Lord Ashbourne
1841	Lord Campbell	1886	John Naish
1841	Sir Edward Burtenshaw Sugden	1886	Lord Ashbourne
		1892	Sir Samuel Walker
1846	Maziere Brady	1895	Lord Ashbourne
1852	Francis Blackburne	1905	Sir Samuel Walker
1853	Maziere Brady	1911	Redmond Barry
1858	Sir Joseph Napier	1913	Ignatius O'Brien
1859	Maziere Brady	1918	Sir James Campbell
1866	Francis Blackburne	1921	Sir John Ross

ATTORNEY GENERAL FOR IRELAND (from 1801, until 1922)

1799	John Stewart	1835	Louis Perrin
1803	Standish O'Grady	1835	Michael O'Loghlen
1805	William Conyngham Plunket	1836	John Richards
1807	William Saurin	1837	Stephen Woulfe
1822	William Conyngham Plunket	1838	Nicholas Ball
1827	Henry Joy	1839	Maziere Brady
1831	Francis Blackburne	1840	David Richard Pigot

1841	Francis Blackburne	1877	Edward Gibson
1842	Thomas Berry Cusack Smith	1880	Hugh Law
1846	Richard Wilson Greene	1881	William Moore Johnson
1846	Richard Moore	1883	Andrew Marshall Porter
1847	James Henry Monahan	1883	John Naish
1850	John Hatchell	1885	Samuel Walker
1852	Joseph Napier	1885	Hugh Holmes
1853	Abraham Brewster	1887	John George Gibson
1855	William Keogh	1888	Peter O'Brien
1856	John David Fitzgerald	1890	Dodgson Hamilton Madden
1858	James Whiteside	1892	The Macdermot
1859	John David Fitzgerald	1895	John Atkinson
1860	Rickard Deasy	1905	James Campbell
1861	Thomas O'Hagan	1905	Richard Cherry
1865	James Anthony Lawson	1909	Redmond Barry
1866	John Edward Walsh	1911	Charles O'Connor
1866	Michael Morris	1912	Ignatius O'Brien
1867	Hedges Eyre Chatterton	1913	Thomas Molony
1867	Robert Richard Warren	1913	John Moriarty
1868	John Thomas Ball	1914	Jonathan Pim
1868	Edward Sullivan	1915	John Gordon
1870	Charles Robert Barry	1916	James Campbell
1872	Richard Dowse	1917	James O'Connor
1872	Christopher Palles	1918	Arthur Samuels
1874	John Thomas Ball	1919	Denis Henry
1875	Henry Ormsby	1921	Thomas Brown
1875	George Augustus Chichester		

SOLICITOR GENERAL FOR IRELAND (from 1801, until 1922)

1801	James McClelland	1830	Philip Cecil Crampton
1803	William Conyngham Plunket	1834	Michael O'Loghlen
1805	Charles Kendall Bushe	1835	Edward Pennefather
1822	Henry Joy	1835	Michael O'Loghlen
1827	John Doherty	1835	John Richards

1836	Stephen Woulfe	1875	David Robert Plunket
1837	Maziere Brady	1877	Gerald FitzGibbon
1839	David Richard Pigot	1878	Hugh Holmes
1840	Richard Moore	1880	William Moore Johnson
1841	Edward Pennefather	1881	Andrew Marshall Porter
1841	Joseph Devonshire Jackson	1883	John Naish
1842	Thomas Berry Cusack Smith	1883	Samuel Walker
1842	Richard Wilson Greene	1885	The Macdermot
1846	Abraham Brewster	1885	John Monroe
1846	James Henry Monahan	1885	John George Gibson
1847	John Hatchell	1886	The Macdermot
1850	Henry George Hughes	1886	John George Gibson
1852	James Whiteside	1887	Peter O'Brien
1853	William Keogh	1888	Dodgson Hamilton Madden
1855	John David Fitzgerald	1890	John Atkinson
1856	Jonathan Christian	1892	Edward Carson
1858	Henry George Hughes	1892	Charles Hare Hemphill
1858	Edmund Hayes	1895	William Kenny
1859	John George	1897	Dunbar Plunket Barton
1859	Rickard Deasy	1900	George Wright
1860	Thomas O'Hagan	1903	James Campbell
1861	James Anthony Lawson	1905	Redmond Barry
1865	Edward Sullivan	1909	Charles O'Connor
1866	Michael Morris	1911	Ignatius O'Brien
1866	Hedges Eyre Chatterton	1912	Thomas Molony
1867	Robert Richard Warren	1913	John Moriarty
1867	Michael Harrison	1913	Jonathan Pim
1868	John Thomas Ball	1914	James O'Connor
1868	Henry Ormsby	1917	James Chambers
1868	Charles Robert Barry	1917	Arthur Samuels
1870	Richard Dowse	1918	John Powell
1872	Christopher Palles	1918	Denis Henry
1872	Hugh Law	1919	Daniel Wilson
1874	Henry Ormsby	1921	Thomas Brown

SECRETARY OF STATE FOR NORTHERN IRELAND

1972   William Whitelaw

1973   Francis Pym

1974   Merlyn Rees

1976   Roy Mason

1979   Humphrey Atkins

1981   James Prior

MINISTER OF STATE

1972-2	Paul Channon	1979-	Michael Alison
1972-3	Lord Windlesham	1981-	Adam Butler
1972-4	William Van Straubenzee	1981-	Lord Gowrie
1972-4	David Howell		
1974-6	Stanley Orme		
1974-6	Roland Moyle		
1976-9	John Concannon		
1976-9	Lord Melchett		
1979-81	Hugh Rossi		

PARLIAMENTARY UNDER-SECRETARY

1972-2	David Howell	1979-81	Lord Elton
1972-4	Peter Mills	1981-	David Mitchell
1973-4	Lord Belstead	1981-	John Patten
1974-6	Lord Donaldson	1981-	Nicholas Scott
1974-6	John Concannon		
1976-9	James Dunn		
1976-9	Raymond Carter		
1978-9	Thomas Pendry		
1979-81	Philip Goodhart		
1979-81	Giles Shaw		

SPEAKER OF THE HOUSE OF COMMONS

1258	Peter de Montfort	1340	William Trussell
1327	William Trussell	1347	William de Thorpe
1332	Henry Beaumont	1351	William de Shareshull
1332	Sir Geoffrey le Scrope	1362	Sir Henry Green

All the above were Presiding Officers of Parliament rather than Speakers of the House of Commons.

1376	Sir Peter de la Mare	1407	Thomas Chaucer
1377	Sir Thomas Hungerford (the first to be designated Speaker)	1413	William Stourton
		1413	John Dorewood
		1414	Sir Walter Hungerford
1377	Sir Peter de la Mare	1414	Thomas Chaucer
1378	Sir James Pickering	1415	Sir Richard Redmayne
1380	Sir John Guildesborough	1416	Sir Walter Beauchamp
1381	Sir Richard Waldegrave	1416	Roger Flower
1383	Sir James Pickering	1420	Roger Hunt
1394	Sir John Bussy	1421	Thomas Chaucer
1399	Sir John Cheyne or Cheney	1421	Richard Baynard
1399	John Dorewood	1422	Roger Flower
1401	Sir Arnold Savage	1423	Sir John Russell
1402	Sir Henry Redford	1425	Sir Thomas Walton or Wauton
1404	Sir Arnold Savage		
1404	Sir William Sturmy or Esturmy	1426	Sir Richard Vernon
		1427	Sir John Tyrrell
1406	Sir John Tiptoft	1429	William Alington

1431	Sir John Tyrrell	1523	Sir Thomas More
1432	Sir John Russell	1529	Sir Thomas Audley
1433	Roger Hunt	1533	Sir Humphrey Wingfield
1435	John Bowes	1536	Sir Richard Rich
1437	Sir John Tyrrell	1539	Sir Nicholas Hare
1437	William Burley	1542	Sir Thomas Moyle
1439	William Tresham	1545	Sir John Baker
1445	William Burley	1553	Sir James Dyer
1447	William Tresham	1553	Sir John Pollard
1449	Sir John Say	1554	Sir Robert Brooke
1449	Sir John Popham	1554	Sir Clement Heigham
1449	William Tresham	1555	Sir John Pollard
1450	Sir William Oldhall	1558	Sir William Cordell
1453	Thomas Thorpe	1559	Sir Thomas Gargrave
1454	Sir Thomas Charlton	1563	Thomas Williams
1455	Sir John Wenlock	1566	Richard Onslow
1459	Sir Thomas Tresham	1571	Sir Christopher Wray
1460	John Green	1572	Sir Robert Bell
1461	Sir James Strangeways	1581	Sir John Popham
1463	Sir John Say	1584	Sir John Puckering
1472	William Alington	1589	Thomas Snagge
1483	John Wood	1593	Sir Edward Coke
1484	William Catesby	1597	Sir Christopher Yelverton
1485	Sir Thomas Lovell	1601	Sir John Croke
1487	Sir John Mordaunt	1604	Sir Edward Phelips
1489	Sir Thomas Fitzwilliam	1614	Sir Randolph Crewe
1491	Sir Richard Empson	1621	Sir Thomas Richardson
1495	Sir Robert Drury	1624	Sir Thomas Crewe
1496	Sir Reginald Bray (Presiding Officer at Great Council)	1626	Sir Heneage Finch
		1628	Sir John Finch
		1640	Sir John Glanville
1497	Sir Thomas Englefield	1640	William Lenthall
1504	Edmund Dudley	1647	Henry Pelham
1510	Sir Thomas Englefield	1647	William Lenthall
1512	Sir Robert Sheffield	1653	Francis Rous
1515	Sir Thomas Neville	1654	William Lenthall

1656	Sir Thomas Widdrington	1761	Sir John Cust
1657	Bulstrode Whitelocke	1770	Sir Fletcher Norton
1659	Chaloner Chute	1780	Charles Wolfran Cornwall
1659	Sir Lislebone Long	1789	William Wyndham Grenville
1659	Thomas Bampfylde	1789	Henry Addington
1659	William Lenthall	1801	Sir John Mitford
1660	William Say (Speaker pro tem)	1802	Charles Abbot
		1817	Charles Manners Sutton
1660	William Lenthall	1835	James Abercromby
1660	Sir Harbottle Grimston	1839	Charles Shaw-Lefevre
1661	Sir Edward Turnour	1857	John Evelyn Denison
1673	Sir Job Charlton	1872	Henry B.W.Brand
1673	Sir Edward Seymour	1884	Arthur Wellesley Peel
1678	Sir Robert Sawyer	1895	William Court Gully
1678	Sir Edward Seymour	1905	James W.Lowther
1679	Sir William Gregory	1921	John H.Whitley
1680	Sir William Williams	1928	Edward A.Fitzroy
1685	Sir John Trevor	1943	Douglas Clifton Brown
1689	Henry Powle	1951	W.S.Morrison
1690	Sir John Trevor	1959	Sir Harry Hylton-Foster
1695	Paul Foley	1965	Horace King
1698	Sir Thomas Littleton	1971	Selwyn Lloyd
1701	Sir Robert Harley	1976	George Thomas
1705	John Smith		
1708	Sir Richard Onslow		
1710	William Bromley		
1714	Sir Thomas Hanmer		
1715	Sir Spencer Compton		
1728	Arthur Onslow		